KT-562-411

CONTENTS

Birds – Spotting and Studying is designed to create an awareness of the birds present in a garden, park, wood or open country, and indicate how they may be studied closely, either by direct observation or by the detection and interpretation of natural clues. It can be used both in the field and at home as a reference book. The species included are mainly those likely to be commonly seen and readily identified by a new birdwatcher, and the book is intended to give a grounding in identification and detective work rather than providing comprehensive coverage of all the birds and signs it may be possible to see.

The book is split into several sections and is designed to lead from the search for general clues and evidence, which can be related to individual species, on to detailed practical study and project work. The information about the animals can be obtained without destroying their homes, surroundings and natural behaviour patterns since it is based on observation and objects the birds have no further use for, such as feeding remains and moulted feathers. Using all the various sections of the book should give a more rounded view of bird behaviour than would be obtained by simply spotting birds.

Clues and evidence, pages 6-9
In two imaginary scenes, the range of clues likely to be found on the ground and above it is shown. This includes footprints, trails, feeding remains, droppings and nests. Study these scenes to become aware of the variety of signs of bird activity and the many different places in which they are found. The examples in the two scenes are explained in detail later in the book.

Observing birds, pages 10-11
These two pages provide information about equipment required and some basic techniques for watching birds in the field. They should be consulted before stalking birds in the countryside.

How birds work, pages 12-13
This deals simply with some general aspects of bird biology, particularly those that have a bearing on the field observations you will be able to make of birds.

Ready reference/Keys section, pages 14-26
This is concerned with determining which species of bird created a particular clue or item of evidence. It is divided into several units.

Types of bird, pages 14-15
These two pages describe the main groups of birds to be seen in this country and some of the characteristics by which you can recognize them. Included is a ready reference table to bird shapes, sizes and colours.

Flight patterns, pages 16-17
This sets out to show some of the different ways that birds move through the air, and helps you identify birds by their characteristic flight.

The Nature Detective Series

BIRDS
Spotting and Studying

John Stidworthy

Illustrated by Alan Harris
Series Editor Lionel Bender

Macdonald

This book was designed and produced
by The Oregon Press Ltd, Faraday House,
8-10 Charing Cross Road, London WC2H 0HG for
Macdonald & Co. (Publishers) Ltd, Maxwell House,
Worship Street, London EC2A 2EN

Series conceived, designed and edited by
Lionel Bender, 10 Chelmsford Square,
London NW10 3AR, assisted by Madeleine Bender

ISBN 0-356-09718-8

Printed and bound by William Collins Sons
& Co. Ltd, Glasgow

Movement patterns, pages 18-19
Here are shown some of the ways that birds move or perch on the ground, in or on trees, or in the water. These will help you identify species by their method of locomotion. There is also a key to some of the bird footprints you may find.

Food remains, pages 20-21
This deals with the main types of plant or animal remains left by birds, and also with pellets and droppings.

Feathers, pages 22-23
These pages reveal how with finds of single feathers it is possible to start deducing which species, and from which part of the bird's body, an item of plumage may have originated.

Nests, pages 24-25
This shows some of the nesting sites used by birds, and has a key which will help you identify the owner of any nest site you have discovered.

Sounds, page 26, deals with the role of sound in bird life and its importance to you the birdwatcher.

Species fact files, pages 27-71
This, the longest section of the book, provides an 'identikit' picture for each of 44 species of bird. There is a description and illustration of the bird, its nest, its flight and, where appropriate, footprints, feeding signs and droppings, as well as concise summary information related to habitat, habits, sounds, diet and range in Europe. The fact files thus provide an in-depth and all-encompassing look at the various individual clues and pieces of evidence highlighted in the earlier sections.

Practical section, pages 72-77
These pages look in detail at keeping a field notebook, making surveys, watching nesting behaviour, and making a collection of clues and evidence. They make suggestions for some nature detective projects and will help to put into practice the theoretical contents of the book.

Recommended bird sites, page 78, lists a number of suitable places to watch birds in Britain and gives addresses of several organizations which are able to provide further information to help with field study.

The *Bibliography,* page 79, includes books which supplement and extend the information contained in this book. An *Index* of the common names of birds discussed in the book is provided on page 80.

Because most birds are relatively easy to see as they fly about, we sometimes forget to look for the signs and clues which will give us a greater knowledge of their lives and daily and seasonal routines. So keep a sharp lookout not only for the animals themselves, but for the signs they leave behind, such as food remains, feathers and footprints, and also for their roosting and nesting sites.

An owl roosts by day close to the trunk of a tree.

Cawing leads to a rookery high in the trees.

Below rook's nests are droppings and pellets with food fragments.

Splashed droppings on gable tiles show where pigeons regularly roost.

Below owl roost are pellets containing the remains of prey.

Swallows flying around garage reveal their nest in the rafters.

Tucked under the eaves is a house martin's nest.

Wren's nest concealed behind ivy in a wall.

Blackbird droppings below a regular perching spot on top of gatepost.

Stone used by a thrush to smash snails.

Holes in lawn made by starlings probing for insects.

Nestbox occupied by a blue tit.

The panorama below and that on pages 8-9 give examples of some of the things you might look for in two areas of countryside. There are many other signs of bird activity to find, and you will discover that with practice you become more skilled at detecting and interpreting them.

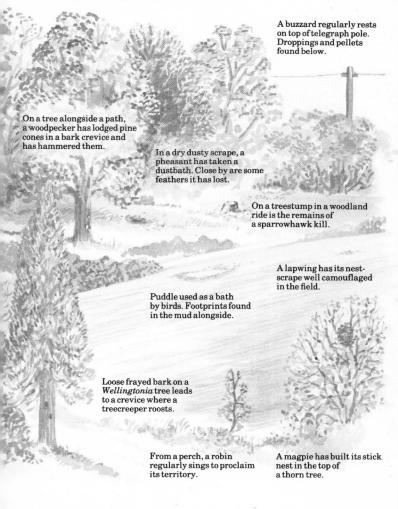

A buzzard regularly rests on top of telegraph pole. Droppings and pellets found below.

On a tree alongside a path, a woodpecker has lodged pine cones in a bark crevice and has hammered them.

In a dry dusty scrape, a pheasant has taken a dustbath. Close by are some feathers it has lost.

On a treestump in a woodland ride is the remains of a sparrowhawk kill.

A lapwing has its nest-scrape well camouflaged in the field.

Puddle used as a bath by birds. Footprints found in the mud alongside.

Loose frayed bark on a *Wellingtonia* tree leads to a crevice where a treecreeper roosts.

From a perch, a robin regularly sings to proclaim its territory.

A magpie has built its stick nest in the top of a thorn tree.

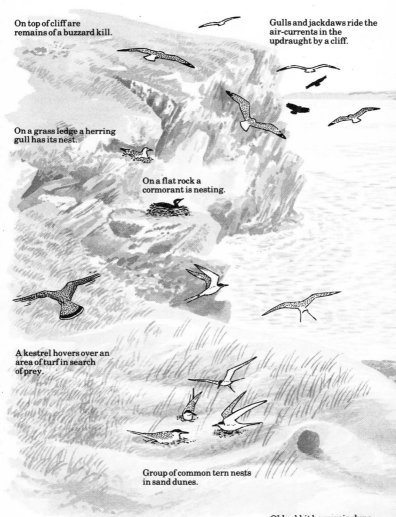

On top of cliff are remains of a buzzard kill.

Gulls and jackdaws ride the air-currents in the updraught by a cliff.

On a grass ledge a herring gull has its nest.

On a flat rock a cormorant is nesting.

A kestrel hovers over an area of turf in search of prey.

Group of common tern nests in sand dunes.

Old rabbit burrow in dune used by shelduck for its nest.

Heronry in trees. The trees are half-dead, splashed with heron droppings. Some heron pellets may be below.

Post sticking out of water is regularly used by cormorants drying their wings.

Sandbank used as resting spot by waders at high tide.

Coot's nest hidden in reeds.

A flock of dunlins feeds at edge of shore.

Swan's nest on banks of lake. Trampled area with droppings is nearby.

Footprints of several types of bird in mud at edge of lake.

Shellfish on a rock have been opened by an oystercatcher.

Oystercatcher's footprints show in damp sand.

Crab eaten by a seagull; its shell is left behind, with beak marks on it.

A heron wades in the shallows.

Seagull footprints lead along the sand.

Cuttlefish bone carries peck marks from a seagull.

To spot birds it is not usually necessary to have elaborate equipment, make great preparations or in any way go to extraordinary lengths. Many birds can be seen in the course of an ordinary walk through the countryside or in a park and no more equipment is needed to find them other than your own eyes and ears. But there are a few simple do's and don'ts if you want to see as many birds as possible. These, together with some general hints, are outlined below.

Stalking behaviour
Do travel quietly. birds can easily be frightened away by sudden noises, crashings in the undergrowth and rustling clothing.

Do not forget to make allowances for the wind. Few birds have much sense of smell so they will not detect your scent on the breeze, but their hearing is good, and the wind can carry your sounds towards them.

Do not create a visual disturbance. Birds' eyesight is good and they may be frightened by flapping clothes, by bright colours, or by a figure moving across the skyline. Wear unobtrusive clothes – greens or browns are good colours – and remember that clothing can provide especially good camouflage if it helps to break up your outline.

Keep off the skyline, do not march across the open unless you have to, and use the cover provided by banks and hedges. But there is no need to take things to extremes – there is rarely much advantage in disguising yourself as a bush and crawling on your belly across the countryside.

If you can, watch birds with the sun behind you or to the side. This makes it easier to see them and distinguish colours.

Vantage points and hides
Often you may see more birds if, instead of moving around, you find a comfortable vantage point, perhaps under a tree or hedge, and sit quiet and still to watch the birds. The dividing line between two habitats, such as woodland and farmland, is often a good place for this because as well as providing you with some shelter and good sight lines, you have the chance of seeing birds from both types of habitat.

Another technique for seeing birds is to use a hide. On bird reserves these are often built overlooking areas where birds congregate and give a marvellous opportunity of watching birds in relative comfort and without disturbing them. For most birdwatching, though, it is not necessary to hide completely, but simply to be quiet and gentle. Birds soon return to an area if they do not feel threatened and are not constantly disturbed.

Using binoculars
It is possible to bird-spot quite satisfactorily using your unaided eyes, but there comes a time when most people feel the need for some help to look more closely at birds. This is the time to buy binoculars. They will allow you to watch more closely what a distant bird is doing, or to home in on fine details of the plumage which may be essential in distinguishing similar species. Opinions differ as to the best magnification power of binoculars for watching birds. Probably $7\times$ or $8\times$ are best to start with; $9\times$ or $10\times$ give greater magnification but a narrower field of view,

making it harder to track a moving bird, and they need more focussing. Binoculars with 7× or 8× magnification are usually smaller and lighter, too, making them better for birdwatching trips. The second figure in a binocular specification, 8 × 40, refers to the light-gathering power, and the higher the better. One last point, a pair of binoculars with centre-wheel focussing is needed. (Do not buy cheap binoculars with wide-angle lenses – image quality is usually poor.)

A golden rule with binoculars is to try them thoroughly before buying, and get a pair with which you feel comfortable. However expensive and optically sound they are, if you find them heavy, awkward to handle, or difficult to fit snuggly to your eyes, avoid them. Comfortable ones get the most use. If you wear glasses, rubber eyecups fitted to the eyepieces may help. If you often watch birds way out on estuaries and marshes, you may like to graduate to a telescope and tripod, but for the average bird-watcher binoculars are quite sufficient.

Birdwatching vantage points

Woodland

Riverbank and lakes

Open country

Seashore

Birds are essentially flying machines and are beautifully adapted for this job. The bones are very light and mostly hollow with a honeycomb structure or narrow struts inside. Instead of heavy jaws with teeth like ours, birds have no teeth and a light horny bill. This is developed into a variety of shapes according to diet. There is a series of air sacs which run through the body and into the bones and these air sacs are part of the vital air-pumping system which feeds a bird's lungs with the oxygen necessary for muscular activity during flight. Flight is a good means of escaping enemies and so some kinds of bird can afford to have a plumage of bright colours for signalling to one another. However, many birds are of sombre colours or are patterned in a way which helps camouflage them.

Flight also gives a bird the possibility of foraging over long distances for food, or regularly travelling backwards and forwards between roosting areas and feeding grounds many kilometres apart, as do species such as starlings and herring gulls. Even longer distances are flown by birds that migrate seasonally. Our summer visitors travel from the Mediterranean region or from far into Africa, using the long hours of daylight in the northern summer to find the insect food with which to rear their broods, leaving again as food and daylight decline in the autumn. Other birds come to us in the winter, leaving the inhospitable Arctic, and return there in the spring.

Flight is a characteristic shared by nearly all birds. Without exception, birds have feathers. They are important for flight and insulation. Feathers are relatively light structures but even so a bird's plumage often weighs more than its skeleton. The different parts of a bird's plumage all have particular names, and some of these are shown on the diagram opposite. The standard names for these parts are well worth learning as you will find them used again and again to give accurate descriptions of birds, even in books such as this, which tries to avoid technical terms.

Another bird characteristic is the laying of eggs. Many species make a nest to contain and protect them. In this country nest building usually takes place only in spring and summer. In many species a nesting territory is established and it is to maintain this, rather than to delight our ears, that many birds are heard singing at this time of year.

Other than for winter visitors, bird populations are likely to be at their highest levels at the end of the summer. Through the winter, and especially late on should there be cold weather and food shortage, mortality takes its toll. For most birds, the average population size is roughly similar from year to year. A bad winter may cut numbers for a while, but they usually build up again. But there is an upper limit. Because of the limitations of food supply and suitable habitat, birds cannot increase in numbers indefinitely. This is why conservation of suitable habitats, and, if possible, creation of new habitats, is so important. The number of individuals and number of different kinds of bird that we can see is governed by the amount of suitable countryside we are able to provide for them.

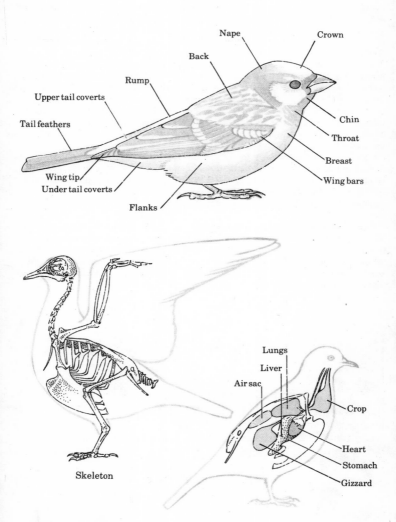

Nape

Crown

Back

Rump

Upper tail coverts

Chin

Tail feathers

Throat

Breast

Wing tip

Wing bars

Under tail coverts

Flanks

Skeleton

Lungs

Liver

Air sac

Crop

Heart

Stomach

Gizzard

Internal organs

Successful bird spotting is really based on categorizing an individual as one of several classic groups – crow, duck, gull, owl, for example – and on comparing one with another as quickly as possible. As you gain experience this becomes easier. These two pages suggests some of the basic things to notice about a bird that will enable you to decide which species it is.

The overall *shape* of a bird is always the first clue. Sometimes it is all you really notice. Wherever possible, note details of the *beak* and *feet*: different groups of birds have different specializations in diet and locomotion which are reflected in the form of these. Note, too, how long the legs are. *Size* is another aid to identification. It can be difficult to estimate the size of a bird in the field, but one way is to become familiar with the appearance of a few common birds at various distances and try to gauge the size of unfamiliar birds in terms of these. In the table here, the blackbird is used as the 'measuring stick'.

Colour is also important in identification. The apparent colour of a bird in the field is not always the same as its actual colour when seen close up. Different levels of light intensity or angles of the sun can play tricks on your colour sense. And the colours you notice may not be the sum total of the colours on the bird. Appreciating such problems is all part of bird spotting.

The table below should help you identify the birds described in this book. It shows **Shape** – overall shape of the bird (most of these shapes correspond to bird families), the shape of the beak and feet – **Size,** compared to a blackbird – medium (M), small (S), large (L), very large (VL), with the first category being the same size as the blackbird, the last category twice the size – and **Colour** – the commonest colours you may notice.

Shape	Beak	Feet	Size	Colour Black	White	Grey	Brown	Blue	Green	Yellow	Orange	Family or species name	See page
			L	●								Coot	28
			L	●	●	●	●		●			Mallard/Duck	29-30
			VL	●								Swan	31
			VL				●					Heron	32
			L		●		●					Grebe	33
			S					●			●	Kingfisher	34
			L/S	●	●							Oystercatcher	35

Shape	Beak	Feet	Size	Black	White	Grey	Brown	Blue	Green	Yellow	Orange	Family or species name	See page
			L	●	●							Lapwing/Dunlin	36-37
			VL	●								Cormorant	38
			L/VL	●	●	●						Gull	39-40
			L/VL			●	●					Sparrowhawk	41-43
			L				●					Tawny owl	44-45
			L/VL	●								Rook	46-49
			M	●								Starling	50
			S				●					Skylark	51
			VL				●		●		●	Pheasant	52-53
			S	●	●							Swallow	54
			S	●			●					Swift	55
			L	●	●	●						Pigeon	56-57
			S		●		●		●			Sparrow/Finch	58-60
			S	●	●	●			●	●		Wagtail	61
			S	●	●				●	●	●	Tit	62-63
			M/L	●	●				●	●		Woodpecker	64-65
			S		●		●					Treecreeper	66
			S			●		●			●	Nuthatch	67
			S				●					Wren	68
			S				●				●	Robin	69
			M	●			●					Blackbird/Thrush	70-71

Some birds have such characteristic ways of flying through the air that it is possible to recognize them at a glance. There are three main things to look for.

(i) The shape or silhouette of the bird in flight. Does it have long, short and round or pointed wings? Does its neck stick out in front or its feet trail behind? Does it have a long tail?
(ii) The way it flaps its wings. Are they beating fast, slowly, or not at all? Are the wingbeats shallow or deep?
(iii) What sort of pattern does its flight make in the air. Does it fly straight and level, or in a bouncy fashion? Does it soar or dive?

Carefully noting these points will help you identify the birds you are watching, and may also give you a clue as to what they are doing – hunting for food, flying to escape enemies, returning to a nest, or just flying from place to place?

This page shows some of the commonest ways in which the birds described in this book fly. Of course, they do not always fly this way. A kestrel is most likely to be seen hovering, but it must flap its wings to get there. More about the flight of each species, including details of special display flights, can be found on the Fact File page as numbered.

Hovering in one spot.

Kestrel p. 41
Skylark p. 51

Soaring, or gliding with little wing movement.

Gulls p. 39-40
Buzzards p. 43
Crows p. 46-49

Straight flight, slow flapping

Heron p. 32
Gulls p. 39-40
Crows p. 46-49

Straight flight, fast wingbeats.

Cormorant p. 38
Pigeons p. 56-57
Thrushes p. 70-71
Kingfisher p. 34
Waders p. 35-37
Starling p. 50
Ducks p. 29-30
Swan p. 31
Grebe p. 33

Fast, swooping flight.

Sparrowhawk p. 42
Swallow p. 54
Swift p. 55

Mixture of fast wingbeats and glides.

Pheasant p. 52
Grouse p. 53

Low and whirring flight.

Coot p. 28
Wren p. 68

Noticeably undulating flight, sometimes closing wings.

Finches p. 58-60
Tits p. 62-63
Nuthatch p. 67
Woodpeckers p. 64-65

Slow, floating flight.

Owls p. 44-45
Lapwing p. 36

Recognizing movement patterns is a good way of identifying birds. On the ground, most of the smaller birds hop, and large birds walk. Crow-size birds usually walk, but may hop, and starlings and thrushes may move in either manner. In trees, woodpeckers and nuthatches have characteristic ways of climbing. On the water, some birds swim with their bodies high, bobbing about on the surface. Others sit much lower in the water.

As well as observing how birds move, notice where they are. Each kind has a place, or range of places, where it is usually found. Tits clamber on the branches and twigs of trees, treecreepers are rarely seen anywhere other than on tree trunks, and so on.

This page shows some of the places you find the birds described in this book, and how they move. Further details can be found on the appropriate page.

Perching in trees
Owls p. 45
Pigeons p. 56-57
Finches p. 58-60
Tits p. 62-63
Thrushes p. 69-71

Acrobatics under branches
Tits p. 62-63

Perching on wires
and posts
Kestrel p. 41
Buzzard p. 43
Owls p. 44-45
Swallows p. 54

Climbing up and down
Nuthatch p. 67

Climbing up trees
Woodpeckers p. 64-65
Treecreeper p. 66

Walking
Lapwing p. 36
Crows p. 46-49

Running
Game birds p. 52-53
Wagtails p. 61

Hopping
Sparrow p. 58

Swimming low in water and
diving
Grebe p. 33
Cormorant p. 38

Wading in water
Heron p. 32
Waders p. 35-37

Swimming high on water
Coot p. 28
Mallard p. 29
Gulls p. 39-40

Even though bird footprints may not be easy to recognize and, because they were not made in mud, soft sand or snow, may not show features such as webs and small back toes, they are interesting to follow and you may well be able to identify at least the type of bird if not the species. Measure the tracks and make notes or sketches of them. Does the foot seem to be webbed or not? How many toes are there? (A bird's foot usually has three toes at the front and one or none at the back.) How are the toes arranged? What is the size of the foot? Was the bird hopping or walking? Does it seem to have been in a hurry, or going in a leisurely fashion with many pauses? Are there signs of feeding near the footprints? The answers to all these questions will give you a clearer idea of what the bird was and what it was about.

Follow down the key until you come to the best description of the track you are investigating. Then refer to the corresponding page(s) for confirmation.

1 **With webbing on toes** _____ go to **2**
  Without webbing _____ go to **4**
2 Webbed to end of toes _____ go to **3**
  Webbed only near base of toes _____ TERN p. 39
3 Four toes in web _____ CORMORANT p. 38
  Three toes in web _____ DUCKS p. 29-30, SWAN p. 31,
                                              GULLS p. 39-40
4 With lobes on the toes _____ COOT p. 28, GREBE p. 33
  Without lobes on toes _____ go to **5**
5 Back toe small or invisible _____ GROUSE p. 53, PHEASANT p. 52
  Back toe similar size to front toes _____ go to **6**
6 Feet more than 12 cm long _____ HERON p. 32
  Feet less than 12 cm long _____ go to **7**
7 Feet large, with obvious pad marks, not much
  angle between front toes _____ CROW family p. 46-49
  Feet less than 5 cm long _____ go to **8**
8 Medium size feet, walking trail showing
  turned-in toes _____ PIGEONS p. 56-57
  Tiny feet, trail showing hopping _____ SPARROWS p. 58, and other
                                       small perching birds p. 59-71

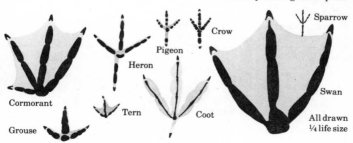

Sparrow
Crow
Pigeon
Heron
Cormorant
Tern
Coot
Swan
Grouse
All drawn ¼ life size

After a meal, a bird may leave behind food remains or feeding signs. If you find these it is often possible to guess which kind of bird has been feeding; each species has a characteristic way of dealing with food. The carcase of a pigeon may reveal that it has been caught by a hawk. An empty nutshell may be obviously the work of a woodpecker. Below are some commonly found feeding signs and remains of food eaten by birds.

Plant remains/signs

Hazelnut with a small hole chipped out and fine beak marks. Great tit p. 63.

Tree bark chipped away to get at insects. Beak marks. Woodpeckers p. 64-65.

Beak marks in rose hips show a bird has been feasting. It is not always possible to say which species but finches p. 59-60 are likely.

Hazelnut chiselled open and emptied. Untidy hole with beak marks. Woodpeckers p. 64-65.

Pine cone with scales hacked off to get at seeds. Woodpeckers p. 64-65.

A walnut hacked open leaving a large irregular hole. Jackdaw p. 49.

Hazelnut hacked open. Small beak marks. Nuthatch p. 67

Animal remains/signs

Bird killed. Breast and head eaten first. Bones not eaten. Feathers lying around. Sparrowhawk p. 42.

Rabbit with fur and skin shreds plucked off. Buzzard p. 43.

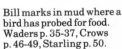

Bill marks in mud where a bird has probed for food. Waders p. 35-37, Crows p. 46-49, Starling p. 50.

Mussels prised open and eaten. Oystercatcher p. 35.

Eggshell, chipped open and contents eaten, left lying on ground. Gulls p. 39-40, Crows p. 46-49.

Broken snail shells. Thrush p. 71.

Droppings Birds generally produce droppings which are a mixture of faeces – remains of food which has passed through the gut – and urine, which in birds is often in the form of a whitish paste. Many birds produce droppings which are more or less indistinguishable from one another – often a mixture of greenish-brown and white pastes. Even these should not be overlooked as useful clues. A sprinkling of droppings may signal the roost of a bird above, or a regular feeding place, or sometimes may give a clue to a nesting place.

Some birds produce more recognizable droppings. Grouse, for example, have droppings which contain remains of some of the fibrous bits of plant they have eaten. Fruit-eating birds may pass in their droppings pips from fruit. Birds that eat large quantities of insects may leave droppings with fragments of insect skeleton in them.

So bird droppings are worth investigating. They may allow you to guess which bird produced them. Alternatively, if you know which bird produced them, you may be able to tell something about its diet.

Insect skeletons –
Green woodpecker p. 64.

Fibrous plant remains –
Grouse p. 53. See also
Pheasant, Partridge p. 52.

Seeds from rose hips –
Blackbird p. 70. Thrush p. 71.

Pellets Some birds get rid of indigestible parts of their food by forming them into a pellet and expelling this through their mouth. The pellet is usually ball- or sausage-shaped and may give a good indication of the bird that produced it and the bird's diet. Many kinds of bird produce pellets, including herons, gulls, crows, kingfishers, curlews and other waders, but the best known are probably those of owls and the daytime birds of prey. Owls swallow their prey whole and do not digest the bones so their pellets are specially good in giving an indication of the birds' diet. Pellets are most likely to be found at roosting sites, or sometimes at spots where a bird has fed.

Bones, fur and sometimes
insect remains – Tawny
owl p. 45. See also Barn
and Little owl, p. 44, 45

Plant, berry or insect remains – Black-headed gull
p. 39. See also gulls p. 39-40.

Mainly fur. Surprisingly,
no fish bones – Heron p. 32.

Pellets mainly of fur or
feathers – Kestrel p. 41.
(Hawks tear off meat to
swallow and may digest
the bones they take in.)
See also p. 42-45.

Plants, grass, insect re-
mains, stones – Rook p. 48.
See also p. 46-49.

Feathers provide birds with both a coat that keeps them warm and aerodynamic surfaces which allow them to fly. Feathers on different parts of the body do different jobs and vary in shape and size. Several main types can be recognized.

Down feathers have very little shaft, but many fluffy branches. They form an insulating layer below the outer feathers. *Contour feathers* are usually short, with a downy base, and help to give the outline to the bird. *Tail feathers* are long, smooth and fairly stiff. Often quite symmetrical, with a central shaft, they are important for steering, braking and balancing in flight. The main *wing feathers* are long and strong and provide the main flying surface. *Primary feathers* are the longest of all. They push the bird through the air. They are often asymmetrical, the trailing section being wider than the leading one. In some birds, such as crows, which have slots (gaps in the wingtip), the feathers are narrower towards the tip of the wings. *Secondary feathers* occur closer to the body and are smaller and more symmetrical. They provide much of the lift for the bird.

Once grown, feathers are dead structures, and they gradually become worn. A new set of feathers is grown each year and the old set is lost. In most birds the change-over of feathers is gradual, flight feathers being lost one at a time so the birds are never grounded. In a few species, such as ducks and grebes, the moult is more sudden and the birds are temporarily flightless in late summer. Generally the moult is at the end of the breeding season.

Bird feathers are a fairly common find. Some provide good clues to their former owners. Below are some of the more distinctive feathers you may detect.

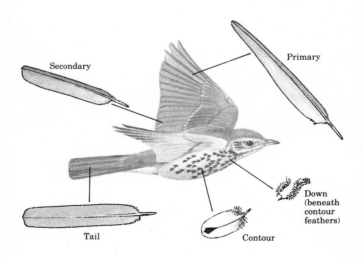

Secondary

Primary

Tail

Contour

Down (beneath contour feathers)

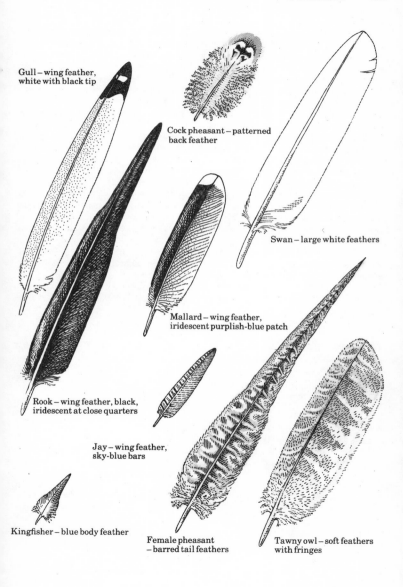

Gull – wing feather, white with black tip

Cock pheasant – patterned back feather

Swan – large white feathers

Mallard – wing feather, iridescent purplish-blue patch

Rook – wing feather, black, iridescent at close quarters

Jay – wing feather, sky-blue bars

Kingfisher – blue body feather

Female pheasant – barred tail feathers

Tawny owl – soft feathers with fringes

Nearly all birds make some sort of nest for the protection of their eggs and young. In most cases it is not a 'home' to which birds return to sleep. At its simplest, a nest is a scrape in the earth, or an already existing hole in a tree. At the other extreme, some birds make elaborate and beautiful nests, bound together with great care out of carefully collected and worked materials. The nest may be nearly flat, or have a well-defined cup to hold the eggs, or even have a roof as well as a base.

Nests are interesting not only in the way they may be constructed and concealed but also because they are the places where some of the most important of the bird's behaviour takes place. Furthermore, they are vital to the continuation of the species. It is well to remember this and to curb your curiosity. Do not knowingly disturb birds on the nest. During the breeding season, stay at a distance. Notice where nests are by all means, but do not poke about near them. There is still plenty to observe – the feeding trips of the adults, their frequency and success, and later, perhaps, the emergence of the fledglings.

After the breeding season has ended the chance comes to examine nests. Many become revealed only as leaves fall in the autumn. If you examine nests before they are damaged in winter storms you can note all the details of their construction. What are the main materials? How are they held together? Is there a distinct lining?

Not only do bird species each have their own style of nest-building, they also have a particular type of site they like to occupy. The page opposite shows some of the main types of bird nesting sites.

The key below will help you to find out some of the birds which commonly use each type of site. More about their nests can be found on the appropriate Fact File pages.

Nest site key

1 In a hole _____ go to **2**
  Not in a hole _____ go to **3**
2 Hole in tree _____ Jackdaw p. 49, Starling p. 50,
             Tits p. 62-63, Woodpeckers p. 64-65, Treecreeper p. 66
  Burrow _____ Shelduck p. 30, Kingfisher p. 34
  Hole or crevice in bank or wall _____ Pied wagtail p. 61
                                         Wren p. 68, Robin p. 69
3 In or alongside fresh water _____ go to **4**
  Not in or by fresh water _____ go to **5**
4 Pile of vegetation on water _____ Coot p. 28, Grebe p. 33
  Nest near the water _____ Mallard p. 29, Mute swan p. 31
5 On cliffs or rocks _____ Cormorant p. 38, Herring gull p. 40
  Not on cliffs _____ go to **6**
6 In or on buildings _____ Barn owl p, 44, Swallow p. 54
               Swift p. 55, Pigeon p. 56, House sparrow p. 58
  Not on buildings _____ go to **7**
7 On the ground _____ go to **8**
  Not on the ground _____ go to **9**

As a whole, birds are quite noisy animals. You have only to venture into a peaceful area of countryside in spring or summer, or go into your garden on a 'quiet' evening, to realize that there can be a real hubbub of bird sounds filling the air.

There are three main types of sounds made by birds:

Songs are rhythmic and often complex sequences of notes which are usually tuneful to the human ear. They are produced by the small perching birds such as tits and finches and are used by them to attract a mate or to proclaim ownership of a territory. In most cases, songs are uttered by the males of a species. For recognition purposes, each species has its own particular song, and this provides humans, too, with a handy sound label for the bird.

Calls are single notes or short groups of notes used for the communication of information. They may be uttered in alarm, on discovery of a good nest site, on finding food, or just to maintain contact with one another. They are produced by many kinds of bird and are often distinctive, although the alarm calls of many species are similar. Calls can be used by humans to help identify birds, and also, with practice, to give an indication of what a bird is doing.

Mechanical sounds produced by birds include wing noise in flight, tappings and scrapings during feeding, splashes during diving, and sounds made while foraging. Many of these sounds are incidental to what the bird is doing, but some, such as woodpecker tapping, may be 'taken over' and used as a means of communication.

Some birds are particularly noisy in their movements and this is noted in the pages which follow. These noises are useful signs. A wood-pigeon taking off from a tree makes an unmistakeable noise, and it is amazing how often a noise in the undergrowth, sounding like a herd of buffalo crashing about in the leaves, turns out to be a blackbird looking for its dinner.

Bird sounds are notoriously difficult to represent in print. Different people hear them in different ways and invent their own 'word-equivalent' for what they hear. But the calls are represented in this book by words which make an approximation to the bird's sound. They are a useful guide to the rhythms and types of sound you will hear. If you are interested in bird sounds, the best tuition in the subject is to get hold of some of the excellent cassette or disc recordings of them which are available nowadays and listen to these over and over again until you are familiar with the various species.

On the following Fact File pages, 44 species of bird are considered in detail. These are by no means all the birds it is possible to see in the British Isles (where there are well over 200 species to be observed), but it does cover most of the commonest birds and those easily recognized by a novice.

All birds included in the book may be seen in Britain, and all occur on the Continent, although sometimes there are regional colour differences; these are noted briefly. Most of the birds described are residents in Britain, but a few are migrants and are here only for part of the year. This, too, is noted in the text. (Some resident species, such as starlings, have their numbers increased in the winter by migrants from Scandinavia.) On some of the pages, in addition to full details of the main species, allied species are briefly described. There are 22 such additional species. All species have been arranged according to natural (scientific) family groupings, and this tends to coincide with their habitats, i.e. seabird's, freshwater and estuarine birds, open country and woodland and garden birds. (Additional species are always illustrated – above (A), below (B), to the left (L) or right (R) of their caption.)

The information on each page is concise but clear and is designed to help you identify a bird either by direct sighting or from its signs. It is presented in the following standard format:

There is a *description* of the bird, including its unique features, colour and size. Mention is made if it is likely to be seen in flocks. An accompanying picture shows the bird in its natural surroundings.

The bird is also illustrated in *flight*, and mention is made of any particular features of its flight pattern. The *nest* and *nest site* are described and illustrated.

Other features are described if they are particularly noteworthy or distinctive. These include *behaviour patterns* or *postures* which are readily seen. If the bird is likely to leave *tracks*, then footprints and trails may be shown. Some particularly distinctive feet are illustrated. In some cases, feeding adaptations are included, and where *food remains*, regurgitated *pellets* or bird *droppings* are likely to be helpful in identification, these, too, are shown.

The text at the bottom of each page gives concise details of *habitat*, explaining the type of country in which the bird lives. *Habits* include where it feeds, movement patterns on the ground, and brief notes on breeding. *Sounds* are noted, both those produced by voice and by movements. A brief outline of the *diet* is given. Finally, there is broad indication of the *range* of the species over the whole of Europe.

A short selection like this obviously poses some problems. For example, visiting a lake or reservoir you may see many kinds of swans and ducks, and also geese, which are not mentioned here. In just a few pages it is impossible to cover all the wildfowl, many of them ornamental, which you may see in such a situation. But as you will know at least the group of birds concerned, it is possible to learn something of the behaviour of another species by studying its close relatives.

Emphasis here has been given to those species and signs which are most easily seen. Many details of habits are omitted, but these, together with other species, detailed distributions, and other less obvious evidence, can be found in books listed in the Bibliography (page 79).

Nest Moored in shallow water, often amongst vegetation. A floating structure of reeds and other aquatic plants, it keeps the eggs above the water.

Description 38 cm long. Appears all black except for the bill and shield on front of head, which are bright white. Looks tail-less. Often occurs in groups, but quarrelsome.

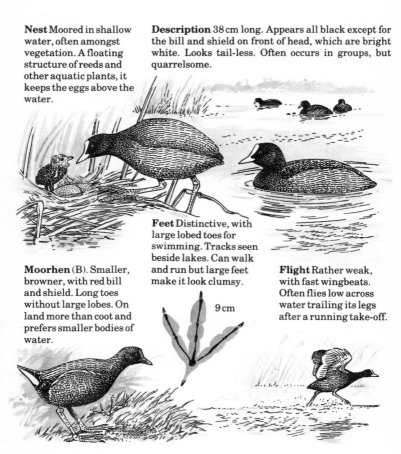

Feet Distinctive, with large lobed toes for swimming. Tracks seen beside lakes. Can walk and run but large feet make it look clumsy.

9 cm

Moorhen (B). Smaller, browner, with red bill and shield. Long toes without large lobes. On land more than coot and prefers smaller bodies of water.

Flight Rather weak, with fast wingbeats. Often flies low across water trailing its legs after a running take-off.

Habitat Usually on lakes and reservoirs.
Habits Good swimmer and diver. Jumps up before diving. Breeds from March to August, laying 6-9 eggs, buff with dark markings.
Sounds Call is a loud, rather metallic sounding 'keuk'. May slap water in flight and has noisy take-off and landing.
Diet Seeds, shoots and roots of water plants, small fish and insects. Most food is obtained by diving.
Range Common resident in most parts. Absent from N. Scandinavia.

Flight Strong flier, with long neck outstretched, feet tucked to body. The wings are set far back and beat fast without being raised high above back. When in group may travel in V-formation.

Description 58 cm long. Female always mottled brown. Male with green head, white neck ring and dark brown breast, except from July to September when dull coloured and more like female.

5 cm

Tufted duck (B). This is one of the commonest of other ducks. Much smaller than mallard. Male black with white sides, female dark brown. Yellow eyes. Tuft droops at back of head. Dives for food – plants and small animals.

Nest Usually hidden in thick cover on the ground, but sometimes in a hollow tree. Typically made of grass and stems with a lining of down.

Feet Three toes in web at front for swimming, small fourth toe behind leaving a round imprint. The toes turn in when walking.

Many species of duck have a characteristic coloured patch of feathers on the wing – a speculum. It is purplish blue in the mallard. (The tufted duck has a white wing bar.)

5 cm

Habitat Lakes, ponds, reservoirs and other freshwater bodies, marshes, estuaries and seawater lagoons.
Habits Good swimmer, riding high on water. Also walks well. May be seen dabbling with beak at surface, or up-ending for food; rarely dives. Breeds from March to May. Lays 8-10 greenish eggs.
Sounds Female makes familiar 'quack', male a quieter, higher note.
Diet Shoots, roots, seeds of water plants. Also snails, insects.
Range Common throughout. Leaves N. Scandinavia for S in winter.

During the late summer many adults depart for moulting grounds leaving 'nursemaids' in charge of several broods of ducklings together.

Nest Usually in an old rabbit burrow, but sometimes in a hollow under thick cover. It is lined with down.

Feet and tracks Typical large duck feet, with three front toes in a web. Duck tracks leading down a burrow belong to a shelduck.

Flight Flies well but not fast, with slower wingbeats than most ducks. Slightly drooping neck and bold pattern, with green speculum, help to identify.

Description 60 cm long. Stands tall, looks and waddles like a goose. Distinctive pattern – dark green head, white throat, chestnut breast, mainly white body. Male has distinct red knob on bill. Sometimes seen in large groups.

Habitat Coastal mudflats, estuaries and sand dunes. Also inland.
Habits May be seen walking and feeding at low tide, but at high tide often standing on shore or swimming. Breeds in May and June, laying 8-14 white eggs.
Sounds In breeding season whistles and deep laughing 'ahg-ahg-ahg' heard.
Diet Small shellfish, shrimps, and vegetable matter.
Range Breeds on coasts of N.W. Europe. Some move S for winter.

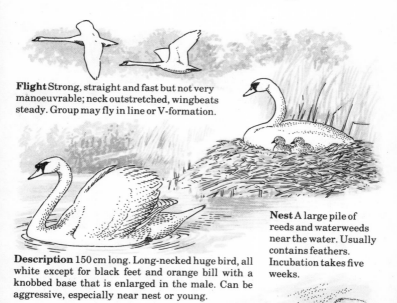

Flight Strong, straight and fast but not very manoeuvrable; neck outstretched, wingbeats steady. Group may fly in line or V-formation.

Nest A large pile of reeds and waterweeds near the water. Usually contains feathers. Incubation takes five weeks.

Description 150 cm long. Long-necked huge bird, all white except for black feet and orange bill with a knobbed base that is enlarged in the male. Can be aggressive, especially near nest or young.

Droppings Greenish cylinders, often with 'cut-off' ends, may be found near resting places on banks and shores. They measure up to 15 cm long and 20 cm across and contain plant remains.

Feet and tracks Very large foot, with front three toes in a swimming web with an almost straight front edge. The bird makes strong impressions but the small hind toe often leaves no mark.

16 cm

Habitat Lakes, rivers, canals, other freshwater; sometimes on sea.
Habits Occasionally on land, but generally seen on water swimming with neck in graceful curve, or dipping head or up-ending for food. Breeds from April to June, laying 5-7 grey-green eggs.
Sounds Not mute. Snorts, hisses and sometimes feeble trumpeting. Noisy flight with loud singing wingbeats.
Diet Mainly water plants. Some grass and small animals.
Range British Isles, Low Countries, Germany and around S. Baltic.

7.5 cm

Flight Very distinctive. Slow but strong. Huge arched wings and slow flapping. Legs and feet trail behind. Head and neck drawn against body.

Feet No webbing, but very long toes spread weight on mud. Large back toe helps in this and also when perching in trees. The track usually shows claw marks.

Description 90 cm long. Long legs, neck and beak but may hunch neck into body. Grey body, lighter head and neck, with black stripe over each eye and black drooping crest. Often keeps very still, both when resting and hunting.

5 cm

Pellets May be found near resting places or under nesting colonies. They vary in shape and size. Fish are usually completely digested, so pellets contain remains of mammal prey – mostly fur – or sometimes feathers or insects.

Nest A large platform of sticks or reeds, lined with smaller twigs and grass. Often in colonies in trees near water, but may also be on the ground in reed beds.

Habitat All kinds of freshwater, marshes and seashore.

Habits Wades in shallows to stalk its prey. Also perches in trees. Breeds from February to June, laying 3-5 blue-green eggs.

Sounds Usual call a harsh 'kraank' when flying, but can also be noisy at nest, croaking and bill-clapping.

Diet Fishes, frogs, voles and rats. Some insects and birds.

Range Widespread, but absent from N. and E. Scandinavia. In S. France in winter only.

Description 47 cm long. Long white neck, pointed pink bill. In summer has a double-tufted crest on top of the head, and a brown frill round the neck, but these are absent in winter, when the bird looks skinnier and whitish.

Little grebe (dabchick) (B). Half the length of the great crested grebe. Appears dark brown and dumpy. On small ponds and slow rivers as well as lakes, usually in places where there is plenty of cover.

Flight Not often seen. Fast and straight, with fast wingbeats. The legs are trailed and the head is carried very low.

Feet The lobed toes are good paddles, and can be folded for the forward part of the swimming stroke. The legs are right at the back of the body – ideal for swimming, but awkward for walking.

Nest A mound of water-vegetation floating on the surface, but usually 'moored' to reeds.

Chicks leave the nest soon after hatching but may be carried some of the time on one parent's back while the other parent dives for food.

Habitat Lakes and reservoirs. May be on coasts in winter.

Habits Swims and dives well; may emerge again some distance from where it submerged. Almost always in water except at nest. Rarely flies. In spring pairs may be seen in elaborate courtship displays. Lays 3-4 white eggs, which soon become stained.

Sounds A growling call. Rattling, moaning noises in courtship.

Diet Small fish, tadpoles, shellfish and some waterweeds.

Range Absent from N. Britain and N. Scandinavia.

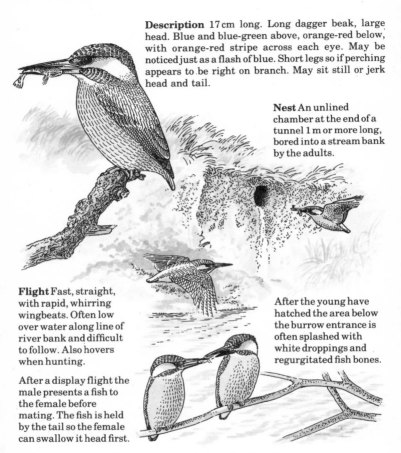

Description 17 cm long. Long dagger beak, large head. Blue and blue-green above, orange-red below, with orange-red stripe across each eye. May be noticed just as a flash of blue. Short legs so if perching appears to be right on branch. May sit still or jerk head and tail.

Nest An unlined chamber at the end of a tunnel 1 m or more long, bored into a stream bank by the adults.

Flight Fast, straight, with rapid, whirring wingbeats. Often low over water along line of river bank and difficult to follow. Also hovers when hunting.

After a display flight the male presents a fish to the female before mating. The fish is held by the tail so the female can swallow it head first.

After the young have hatched the area below the burrow entrance is often splashed with white droppings and regurgitated fish bones.

Habitat Ponds, lakes, canals and slow-flowing rivers.
Habits Plunges from perch after prey; returns to eat, banging prey and then swallowing it head first. Breeds March to August. Lays 6-7 shiny white rounded eggs, usually twice a year.
Sounds A loud whistling 'chee-kee' call. Trilling song.
Diet Small fish such as minnows, also tadpoles, insects.
Range Not in N. Scotland and N. Scandinavia. Otherwise widespread but numbers drop badly after harsh winters.

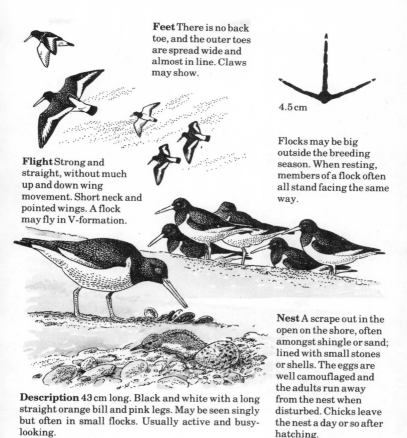

Feet There is no back toe, and the outer toes are spread wide and almost in line. Claws may show.

4.5 cm

Flight Strong and straight, without much up and down wing movement. Short neck and pointed wings. A flock may fly in V-formation.

Flocks may be big outside the breeding season. When resting, members of a flock often all stand facing the same way.

Nest A scrape out in the open on the shore, often amongst shingle or sand; lined with small stones or shells. The eggs are well camouflaged and the adults run away from the nest when disturbed. Chicks leave the nest a day or so after hatching.

Description 43 cm long. Black and white with a long straight orange bill and pink legs. May be seen singly but often in small flocks. Usually active and busy-looking.

Habitat Open shores and estuaries. Some breed inland.
Habits Usually keeps in the open and feeds along sea edge. Probes in mud for food, prises or hammers shellfish from rocks. Breeds April to July. Lays 2-3 buff eggs with dark markings.
Sounds Call is a loud 'bleek-a-bleek', alarm a loud 'cleep, cleep'.
Diet Mussels, cockles, other shellfish, also crabs and worms.
Range Common on most European coasts. Also found inland in Scotland and S. Sweden.

When on the move over some distance the flight is steady and the birds may travel in large irregular flocks.

Flight Flies with slow wingbeats on very broad wings with rounded ends. Can be highly acrobatic, with tumbles and side-slips, as in the breeding season display flight.

Description 30 cm long. Black above and on breast, white below. Spiky, backward-pointing crest and short bill. Usually in flocks.

Parents sometimes put on a show to distract an enemy away from their young. They move on the ground as if they have broken wings.

Nest A scrape on open ground, lined with scraps of plants. The eggs are well camouflaged and the young leave the nest shortly after hatching.

Habitat Arable farmland, also pastures, moors and marshes.
Habits Runs or walks a few paces, then tips forward to pick food from the ground. Breeds March to June. Lays 4 darkish brown eggs with darker markings.
Sounds The call is the 'pee-wit', which gives the bird its other name. Also makes 'lapping' noise in display flight.
Diet Beetle larvae, caterpillars, worms and spiders.
Range Common in most areas but absent from some of Scandinavia.

Description 18 cm long. Long, pointed, slightly downcurved bill. Body grey-brown above, white below in winter. Brown with darker markings in summer, with black belly and white under tail. Usually seen in large flocks.

Flight Flocks fly low and fast over the shore, twisting, climbing, and losing height again. A flock appears almost to flow, changing colour as the birds' upper or lower sides are seen.

Redshank (B). 28 cm long. Red legs, red base to straight beak, and speckled brown body. Alert and noisy. Common on marshes and wet moors. Winter flocks may be on seashore.

Nest A little hollow in a tussock of grass, lined with grass or leaves.

Curlew (L). 55 cm long. Distinctive, long downcurved bill, used to probe down into mud and sand flats. Speckled body. Roosts and nests inland on moors and marshes.

Habitat Shores and estuaries. Breeds near water on moorland.
Habits Probes the ground for food in a hunched-up attitude. Breeds in May and June, laying 4 brown to blue-green eggs.
Sounds A rasping 'treee' as it flies off. A rushing noise from the wings may be heard as a flock flies by.
Diet Small insects, crustaceans, snails, worms and plants.
Range Common on most coasts in winter. In summer on Baltic and Norway coasts; also seen and breeds inland in N. and W. Britain.

Flight Flies fast and straight low over the sea. Sometimes glides. Also seen high in the air travelling in line or V-formation within flocks.

Shag (R). Smaller than cormorant, with no white chin, but with tufted crest. Also perches with wings stretched out. Nearly always on rocky coasts.

Description 90 cm long. Black all over except for white chin; in much of Europe most of the head is white. Rather ungainly-looking. Swims with body on surface or with just back, head and neck showing. The head is often tilted up.

Nest A mound of seaweed, sticks or whatever is available, on a rocky ledge near the sea. On the Continent often nests in trees.

Cormorants often perch on rocks or posts with their wings stretched out as though drying them.

Feet An unusual foot, all four toes joined in the swimming web.

Habitat Most coasts. Also estuaries, reservoirs and lakes.
Habits A good swimmer which dives for fish. May swim some distance underwater. Breeds from April to August. Lays 3-5 pale to blue eggs.
Sounds Mostly quiet, but may growl and croak during breeding.
Diet Fish living on or near the bottom such as flatfish.
Range Absent from E. Baltic and W. Mediterranean, otherwise may be seen on most European coasts and inland in places.

Description 38 cm long. Grey on back and wings, black wingtips. The rest of the feathers are white except for the dark brown head and face (in summer) or dark 'ear' spots (in winter). Feet and beak are red. Often in large flocks.

Flight A buoyant, floating flight on pointed wings. Often glides and wingbeats are slow and not very regular.

Nest A scrape in sand or shingle, or a flattened area of vegetation lined with grass on boggy ground. Usually in colonies.

Pellets Produced at resting places, they may be round or long. Those containing animal remains often crumble apart, but if they contain plants they stick together more.

3 cm

2 cm

Common tern (R). Grey on back and wings, black on top of head, but slimmer than black-headed gull. Narrow pointed wings and forked tail. Dives into the sea for small fish. A tern's footprint shows only a small area of web between the front three toes.

2.5 cm

Habitat Town refuse tips. Reservoirs. Farmland especially where ploughed. Coasts. Sand dunes and moors when breeding.

Habits Often seen far from the sea, being an adaptable bird that uses man by scavenging refuse or following tractors for food. Breeds April to July. Lays 3 eggs, brown with dark markings.

Sounds Quite noisy. Usual call a harsh 'quarrk'.

Diet Offal, worms, insect larvae, fish, crabs, snails, berries.

Range Common generally but does not reach N. Scandinavia.

Flight A powerful flier which often glides and soars in air currents. When travelling it flies slowly, with little up and down movement of the wings.

Description 56 cm long. Tough-looking, with a yellow bill with a red spot near the tip, yellow eyes and pink feet.

Nest A bulky cup of seaweed or grass, most often on cliffs, where turf ledges are preferred, but also nests on the ground or even on buildings.

4 cm

Common gull (R). Smaller and daintier-looking, with distinctive dark eyes and greenish-yellow legs and bill with no red. At coasts and inland, especially in winter, but generally not so common.

Feet and tracks The large feet have three toes in the swimming web, each with a definite claw, but the back toe is small and does not leave a mark. It walks, without the exaggerated turning-in of toes seen in ducks.

Habitat All coasts. Also inland, especially in winter.
Habits A powerful bird. Grabs food away from others, even its own species. Follows boats, hangs around ports, and feeds on rubbish tips, swallowing material with no food value which is later regurgitated. Breeds April to July. Lays 3 green-brown eggs with dark markings.
Sounds A loud 'keeow, keeow' and other screaming cries.
Diet Fish, shellfish, refuse, eggs, chicks and carrion.
Range Extremely common round all N. European coasts.

Flight Able to hover absolutely stationary, flying just sufficiently to compensate for the wind. Hovers several metres up, then flies or glides a short distance and hovers again. Can chase prey, but usually drops on it from the hover. The tail is fanned when hovering, but closed when flying along.

Nest Makes none of its own, but may lay in old nests of other birds – mostly crow and magpie – in trees or on buildings, cliffs or on the ground.

Pellets Found at resting places. Round at one end and pointed at the other, the pellets often contain bits of insects as well as rodents' fur.

Feet Adapted for grasping and killing, with sharp claws.

4 cm

Description 34 cm long. Long pointed wings and long tail. Male has grey head and upper tail, spotted red-brown back and lighter underside. Female is slightly larger and barred brown.

Habitat Open country, motorway verges, sometimes in towns.
Habits Perches on wires and telegraph poles, but most often searches for prey by hovering and scanning the ground below. Breeds April to July. Lays 4-5 whitish eggs with red markings.
Sounds Often quiet, but call is a shrill 'kee-kee-kee'.
Diet Voles and mice, beetles, worms, some small birds.
Range Common throughout most of Europe, but only a summer visitor to N. Scandinavia.

Flight Sometimes soars before selecting hunting area, with wings and tail fanned out. When hunting flies low down one side of hedge then flips over to suprise sparrows/finches.

Nest A rather flat untidy structure of sticks and leaves high in a tree. Often uses an old nest as a basis. Lined with down.

Description Female 37 cm, male 30 cm. Broad rounded wings and long tail, barred appearance below. Head looks small and neck short in flight. Male reddish below, grey above. Female grey-brown above, lighter below.

Bird carcases with plucked feathers lying around are signs of hawk feeding. Raised sites are often used. Heads and breasts of prey are eaten first. Plucked feathers may be marked by the hawk's beak.

3 cm

Pellets Under resting places at the edge of woods. Consist of small feathers packed together and occasionally fur.

Habitat Woods and forests with clearings. Sometimes in open.
Habits Hunts along woodland paths or edges or hedgerows at low level and takes its prey by surprise. As well as speed it has great manoeuvrability. Breeds from May to July, laying 4-6 white, blotched eggs.
Sounds A high chatter – 'kek-kek-kek' – and mewings.
Diet Mainly small birds – in particular finches and sparrows – but also insects and mice.
Range Moderately common, but has suffered from pesticides.

Flight Usually seen soaring. The big broad wings are rounded at the tip, but gaps often show between feathers. Sometimes seen hovering or in slow heavy forward flight.

Nest Usually high in a tree close to the trunk but sometimes on a high cliff ledge, the nest is a large flat platform of sticks lined with other scraps of plants. An old nest may be re-used or added to.

Pellets The large pellets are found under posts and branches on which the bird rests. They usually consist of tightly packed fur.

5 cm

Rabbit carcases surrounded by torn-off tufts of fur and skin may be found where a buzzard has been feeding.

Description 57 cm long. Mainly brown with barring below and some lighter patches, but variable. Seen soaring or perched on wayside poles.

Habitat Heaths, coasts, moors, wooded areas with fields.

Habits Rides air currents for hours, circling in the sky on the lookout for food. May ascend almost out of sight, but pounces on prey from low altitude. Breeds from April to July, laying 2-3 white eggs with dark markings.

Sounds Call is a mewing somewhat high pitched 'keee-oor'.

Diet Rabbits, carrion. Some voles, birds and beetles.

Range Mostly common, but rare in E. Britain.

Flight Low silent hunting flight, rather slow and floating. May make several forays in succession, returning to the same perch.

Description 35 cm long. Heart-shaped white face. White breast (buff on Continent). Looks very pale in flight. Stands upright when perched on long legs, which look knock-kneed. Flies at night and sometimes late afternoon.

3.5 cm

Pellets Spheres or short cylinders found in barns, churches and ruins. They have a shiny, smooth, dark grey appearance. They contain the bones and fur of prey such as mice and shrews.

Nest No nest is built. Eggs are laid on a ledge or the floor in a barn, loft, church tower or ruin, or in a hollow tree. The laying area is often carpeted with pellets.

Habitat Fields, farms, marshes and open country.

Habits Flight is completely silent, allowing it to approach prey easily. Can hunt in complete darkness by listening for prey. Usually breeds in April and May, laying 4-6 white eggs. Eggs hatch every other day so young of different ages.

Sounds Unearthly shriek. Also wheezes and 'snores' at nest.

Diet Mice, shrews, voles and rats. Some birds and insects.

Range Moderately common, but absent from most of Scandinavia.

Flight Fairly fast, straight and low, not floating. Can manoeuvre well through trees.

Nest Usually uses a hollow tree, but occasionally crows' nests or squirrel dreys. The hollow is not lined with nesting material.

Description 38 cm long. Brown with streaks and mottling. A large round head with a big 'face', and broad round wings.

5 cm

Pellets Bumpy-looking grey cylinders, tapered at one end. Bones and fur of mice and voles, parts of birds and insects may be within. Found below trees where the owl roosts.

A gathering of small birds making a lot of noise can lead you to the roosting place of an owl which has been discovered by them and is being 'mobbed'.

Little owl (L). Very small and rather flat-headed. May be seen by day perched on posts or rocks. The flight is very up and down.

Habitat Woods, parks and gardens with trees.
Habits. Flies by night, roosts by day in a tree, often well hidden. Often hunts by watching and listening from a perch, then diving on to prey. Breeds from March to June, laying 2-4 white, somewhat short oval or almost spherical eggs.
Sounds Hoots 'tu-whit-tuwhoo'. Also often calls 'keee-wick'.
Diet Mostly mice and voles. Some birds, worms and insects.
Range Very common. Absent from Ireland and N. Scandinavia.

Flight The long tail and rather short, rounded wings give a distinctive silhouette. The flight is slow and weak, with a rather moth-like flapping action interspersed with glides.

Nest Usually in a tall tree, the nest is built with sticks and has a lining of mud and small roots. It has a roof and an entrance in the side.

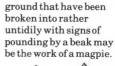

Description 43 cm long, of which half is tail. Striking pied pattern of black and white. When close the black shows glossy blues and greens.

Nuts found on the ground that have been broken into rather untidily with signs of pounding by a beak may be the work of a magpie.

4 cm

Pellets May be found near the nest. Contents include bones and fur, plant remains and grit.

Habitat Farmland and open country with trees and hedges.
Habits Often seen in pairs or small groups. Rather wary, keeping to treetops or flying away if approached. Walks and hops on the ground, holding long tail clear of the surface. Breeds March to June, laying 5-8 greenish eggs with dark markings.
Sounds Call is a fast, rather harsh 'chak-chak-chak-chak'.
Diet Insects, including larvae, fruit, seeds, mice, carrion. Also notorious as predator on eggs and young of other birds.
Range Common throughout all Europe.

Nest Hidden in a tree or bush, the bowl-shaped nest is woven from twigs then lined with hair or fine roots.

Flight Rather weak and slow flight on broad, rounded wings.

In the autumn, jays bury surplus acorns. Later, in the winter, they may return to dig them up and eat them.

Description 34 cm long. Mainly pinkish-brown, but the tail is black with a white rump patch. Black and white wings, with a flash of blue feathers on the shoulders. Feathers on the head may be raised or lowered. Alert and wary.

Habitat Woodland. Also well-wooded farms, parks and gardens.

Habits Finds food both on the ground and in trees. Quick to give alarm call when disturbed. Breeds from April to June, laying 5-6 greenish eggs with olive marks.

Sounds Noisy, harsh voice. Commonly screeches 'skaark, skaark'.

Diet Omnivorous. Eggs, chicks, beetles, grubs, worms and other small animals, acorns, berries, fruit, garden produce.

Range Common throughout Europe, except N. Scotland and N. Scandinavia. Birds in N migrate S in winter.

Flight A fairly smooth, straight flight, often in loose, rather irregular flocks.

Nest In colonies with others in the tops of tall trees, the untidy nest is made of sticks with some mud, and lined with leaves or grass.

Pellets Similar to those of the jackdaw.

Description 46 cm long. Black except for bare, light-coloured area on face. A fairly slender pointed bill. Feather 'trousers' on the thighs. Often in large flocks.

Habitat Farmland with trees.

Habits Gregarious, nesting in colonies ('rookeries') and flying and feeding in groups. Often on fields, picking and probing at ground for food. Breeds March and April, laying 4-6 grey-green or blue eggs with brown marks.

Sounds Usual call a nasal 'caw', but makes other sounds.

Diet Insects, grubs, worms, snails, carrion, seeds, fruit.

Range Mostly common, but absent from N. Scandinavia and S.

Carrion crow. Thicker beak than rook and no bare area on face. Two forms – carrion crow, all black, found in W. Europe and S. Britain; hooded crow, with grey back and breast, found in E. and N. Europe. Seen singly or in small groups. Slow wingbeats, broad wings, and often seeming to go sideways when flying.

Flight Fairly fast wingbeats and in a direct line, often in irregular flocks. Soars and performs aerobatics around cliffs.

Nest A pile of sticks, lined with wool, usually in a hole in a tree, cliff or building but also in chimneys. Often near other jackdaws.

Pellets May be found beneath nests. Contents vary with food but often contain plant remains and small stones.

3 cm

Description 33 cm long. Black, with greyer feathers on the neck and sides of face. The light-coloured eyes are distinctive. Often seen in small groups or larger flocks.

Feet and tracks Jackdaws, rooks and crows have four well developed toes and claws. The front three toes are not widely spread out. On the ground the birds walk not hop.

Habitat Fields near woods, cliffs, farms, villages, towns.
Habits Alert and active, with an upright strutting walk. Often feeds in fields in company with rooks and starlings, as well as other jackdaws. Breeds in April and May, laying 4-6 blue eggs with dark marks.
Sounds Often calls, a ringing 'jack'.
Diet Insects, grubs, worms, eggs, chicks, seeds, fruit.
Range Common in most of Europe. Absent from N. Scandinavia.

Singing from a perch, a starling often droops its wings by its side and flutters them. It sings with a puffy throat.

Nest In a hole in a tree, or a crevice in a wall or under eaves. Made of straw, it may be lined with feathers or fine grass. Often other starling nests are close by.

Flight Fast and straight, sometimes gliding. The wings are pointed triangles, the short tail fan-shaped. Often flies in tight flocks that manoeuvre in unison.

Starlings sometimes find food by keeping close to cattle or sheep and feeding on insects disturbed by their feet. They probe the ground with an open bill. Starlings often cling to sheep, finding food on them.

Description 21 cm long. Appears mainly black, but close to is glossy with lighter markings. More spotted in winter. Perches and stands upright.

Habitat Woods, farms, parks, gardens. May roost in buildings.
Habits Active, noisy, and sometimes quarrelsome. May be seen waddling about on fields and lawns probing at the ground for food. Hops and walks. Often seen in flocks, sometimes huge ones when on way to roost. Breeds from April to June, laying 4-6 pale blue eggs.
Sounds Very varied. A good mimic. Common call a 'tchurr'.
Diet Insects and their larvae, worms, other small animals and scraps. Also berries, fruits.
Range Common. Leaves E. Europe and N. Scandinavia for British Isles in winter.

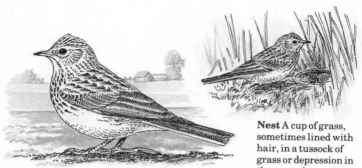

Nest A cup of grass, sometimes lined with hair, in a tussock of grass or depression in the ground.

Description 18 cm long. Brown with darker streaks except on belly, which is pale. The short crest on the head is sometimes raised. The tail is white-edged. Very long hind toes. Walks rather crouched. Difficult to see on the ground, but the song flight is noticeable.

Flight Speedy, with ups and downs with a burst of wingbeats, then closes its wings for a moment. White wing edges clear.

In the song flight it rises almost vertically, may hover for a while in one spot high up, sometimes almost out of sight, then plummets earthwards with wings closed. The bird sings throughout. At times in this flight it appears to 'have its brakes on', wings flapping and tail spread down.

Habitat Arable farmland especially, but most open country.
Habits Feeds on the ground and often flies low, except in the high song-flight. May be present in large numbers and forms flocks outside the breeding season. Breeds from April to July, laying 3-4 white eggs heavily marked with brown.
Sounds A very long, liquid warbling song, usually when on the wing. Call is a 'chirrup'.
Diet Weed seeds, grain, insects and grubs, worms, spiders.
Range Common throughout. Leaves E. Europe and N. Scandinavia for the S in winter.

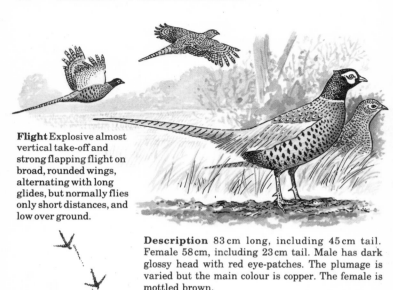

Flight Explosive almost vertical take-off and strong flapping flight on broad, rounded wings, alternating with long glides, but normally flies only short distances, and low over ground.

Description 83 cm long, including 45 cm tail. Female 58 cm, including 23 cm tail. Male has dark glossy head with red eye-patches. The plumage is varied but the main colour is copper. The female is mottled brown.

7 cm

Feet and tracks Often use the same path, and leave well-formed tracks when walking on soft ground. The three front toes are long and thin, the back toe is small.

Droppings Often dark green with one white end, they may be found where pheasants have been feeding, or sometimes a pile of them may give away a roosting site.

Nest A scrape on the ground, lined with a little grass, often well-hidden in thick cover.

Habitat Woods, plantations and fields with cover nearby.
Habits Spends its time feeding on the ground, but roosts on a perch. If disturbed usually runs to cover rather than flying away. Breeds April to June, laying 8-15 olive-brown eggs.
Sounds Males crow 'korr-kok' frequently in spring.
Diet Seeds, fruits, leaves, insects and grubs, worm.
Range Common, but absent from N. Scandinavia. Many reared by man.

Nest A scrape with plant scraps for lining, usually hidden in cover. The young leave the nest soon after hatching.

Feet and tracks Grouse have feathered feet, giving their prints a fat, blurred outline.

4.5 cm

Flight Noisy take-off. Fast, low and straight flight with tipping glides in between rapid wingbeats. The wings are arched when gliding.

Partridge (A). 30 cm long. Rather round, with short wings. On farmland and heaths. Fast smooth runner. Reluctant to fly.

Description 38 cm long. In the British race (red grouse) the male is dark reddish-brown and the female paler but more barred. The Continental race (willow grouse) is all white in winter and has varying amounts of white through the year.

Habitat Moorland.
Habits Walks on the ground, usually keeping low down and concealed in heather. Breeds April to June, laying 4-10 blotched brown eggs.
Sounds Cackling calls 'kowkok-ok-ok-ok'. Whirring flight.
Diet Shoots of heather. Buds and berries.
Range Red grouse in N. England, Wales, Scotland, Ireland. Willow grouse in Scandinavia and eastwards.

House martin (R). Smaller than swallow. White below and white rump, otherwise blue-black. No red. Tail forked but short. Slightly stuttering flight. Builds mud nests, often in colonies, under eaves of buildings.

Flight Fast, with swoops and turns, looking smooth and effortless. Flies low.

Nest On a ledge or rafter inside a barn or similar building, a saucer-shaped nest of mud and dried grass lined with feathers. Swallows may return to the same site year after year.

Description 19 cm long. Dark blue above, pale underneath, red on face and throat; often looks black. A forked tail with long outer feathers. Usually in groups.

Habitat Open farmland; often flies over water.

Habits May be seen perched on wires or roofs, but mostly in graceful flight. Usually produces two broods of 4-5 white eggs with dark markings between May and September.

Sounds Call a high 'twsit-twsit', song a rapid twittering.

Diet Flying insects, mostly caught near the ground.

Range Common throughout except N. Scandinavia. Migrates S to Africa in winter.

Flight Very fast, with fast flickering wingbeats and glides. The wings are kept rather stiff. May fly extremely high, even out of sight, but also hurtles around buildings and down near the ground in the evening or in dull weather. Circles up at dusk, sleeping on the wing.

Nest Straw, grass and feathers are stuck together with saliva to make the saucer-shaped nest in a crevice in a building or rocks.

Description 16.5 cm long. Dark brown, appearing all-black. Long, narrow, swept-back pointed wings. Always in the air except at nest. In flocks.

Habitat The air, especially in areas rich in insects such as over lakes, ponds and marshes.

Habits Spends nearly all its life in flight. Small parties may be seen in what appear to be high-speed chases. Breeds from May to August, laying 2-3 white eggs. Pairs for life, and returns again and again to same area.

Sounds Call is a shrill screaming.

Diet Flying insects such as flies and moths.

Range Common throughout, but migrates S to Africa for winter.

56   **Feral pigeon**   *Columba livia*

Flight Fast and straight once in the air. Rather clattering take-off. Usually flies fairly low. Also seen 'sailing' with wings slanted upwards.

Description 33 cm long. Usually grey, with a darker head, and bars and dark tips on the wings, but can be black, bluish, brown, white or parti-coloured. May be in large flocks.

Nest Pieces of twig or straw in a crevice or on a ledge of a building.

Sharp-eyed and alert, a pigeon may only need to be fed twice by the same person before recognizing him as a useful source of food and flying to him when seen again.

During courtship the male coos and displays to a female by puffing out his neck and making his feathers stand on end. Often the female seems to be trying to ignore him.

Habitat Cities, town, farms. (Wild form on rocky sea cliffs).
Habits Bold and tame in some streets and parks. Waddles along taking food from the ground. Can breed in towns all year, but mainly does so in summer, laying 2 white eggs.
Sounds Calls 'oo-ru-coo'.
Diet Seeds, bread, scraps. Mainly vegetable matter.
Range Common throughout, wherever man is found.

Flight Powerful, fast and direct, with deep wingbeats. Deeply undulating display flight with a noticeable wing clap at the top of a 'wave' and gliding down on stiff wings.

Feet and tracks All four toes are quite large. The bird walks 'pigeon-toed', the front of the feet turned in.

5 cm

Nest A flimsy platform of twigs in a tree, sometimes on a ledge. May be so thin that eggs can be seen from below.

Collared dove (B). 28 cm long. Delicate-looking. Sandy colour with black collar at back of neck. In suburbs and parks. Originally from W. Asia, still spreading in W. Europe. Call is 'coo-cooo, cu'.

Description 40 cm long. Tubby-looking, but the head is relatively small. Mostly grey, but there is an obvious white patch on each side of the neck, and white bars on the wings are seen in flight. Pink breast. Often in big flocks.

Habitat Farmland, woods and, increasingly, parks and towns.
Habits Roosts in trees. Feeds in trees and in flocks on fields. Breeds all year, but mainly August and September, laying 2 white eggs.
Sounds Soft call 'cooo-coo, coo-coo, cu'. Loud clapping of wings on take-off. Wings often whistle in flight.
Diet Grain, seeds, leaves of crops. Berries and buds in trees.
Range Common, but leaves Scandinavia for S in winter.

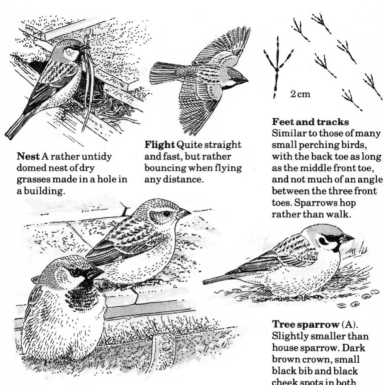

Nest A rather untidy domed nest of dry grasses made in a hole in a building.

Flight Quite straight and fast, but rather bouncing when flying any distance.

Feet and tracks Similar to those of many small perching birds, with the back toe as long as the middle front toe, and not much of an angle between the three front toes. Sparrows hop rather than walk.

2 cm

Tree sparrow (A). Slightly smaller than house sparrow. Dark brown crown, small black bib and black cheek spots in both sexes. Feeds on ground in cultivated areas, but roosts and nests in trees, not usually close to man.

Description 15 cm long. Male grey on top of head, black around eyes and down throat. Brown streaks above, grey-fawn below. Female without black throat, and has a pale streak over eyes.

Habitat In and around human habitation.
Habits Noisy and gregarious. Feeds in towns, gardens, and also in flocks in fields. Breeds mostly from April to August, laying 3-5 white eggs with brown and grey blotches.
Sounds A variety of cheeps and chirrups. Loud and continual.
Diet Almost anything edible – seeds, bread, scraps, insects.
Range Common wherever man and buildings are present.

Flight A succession of rapid wingbeats, followed by closing the wings completely, then more wingbeats, producing a characteristic bounding flight, calling as it goes.

Nest Neatly made of grass, mosses and fibres, covered with lichens and cobwebs, and lined with hair. In a tree, bush or hedge.

♂

♀

Greenfinch (A). 14 cm long. Green with yellow patches on wings and tail. A large bill. In gardens and farmland.

Goldfinch (A). 12 cm long. Red face, yellow bars on wings. Often in small flocks. A 'dancing' up and down flight. Feeds on seeds, especially weeds such as thistles.

Description 15 cm long. Male grey on top and back of head, a pink face and breast. Female is duller, greenish-brown. Both sexes have a greenish rump, and double white bars on wings. The outside of the tail is white. May be in flocks, also mixed with other finches.

Habitat Woods, gardens, parks. Farmland with hedges.
Habits Flocks may be seen feeding on stubble fields. Also hunts for food on the ground in woods. Breeds from April to June, laying 4-5 eggs with red-brown blotches.
Sounds Call a loud 'chwink', repeated. The song is strong and crisp.
Diet Seeds, berries, some insects. Scraps in gardens.
Range Very common throughout Europe.

Description 14.5 cm long. Large head and no distinct neck. Black cap and face. Male has bright pink cheeks and breast, grey back. Female with fawn-coloured underparts.

Flight Rather weak and slow, with a gentle wave-like flightpath. Rounded wings.

Nest A platform of twigs, moss and lichens, lined with rootlets and hair. Well hidden in hedges, brambles or thickets.

Hawfinch (R) 18 cm long. Very large and powerful bill which can crack the stones of cherries, sloes and haws. Also feeds on other fruits and berries. Not very common, usually staying high in the trees, but when on the ground it hops heavily. Not in Scotland, Ireland or N. Scandinavia.

Habitat Woods, gardens, orchards and hedgerows.
Habits Rather shy. Feeds mainly in trees and bushes and less often on the ground. May sometimes be a pest in fruit orchards. Seen in pairs. Breeds from April to July, laying 4-5 green-blue eggs with sparse spots.
Sounds Call is a soft 'peeu'.
Diet Buds, flowers, berries, seeds, some insects.
Range Fairly common in W. and N. Europe.

Flight Buoyant, bounding flight with, periodically, closed wings. Will spring into air to catch a flying insect.

Nest A hole in a wall, rocks or thatch, lined with hair, wool and feathers.

Yellow wagtail (B). Largely yellow (but grey-headed on Continent). Feeds on farmland and marshes, often on insects attracted or stirred up by farm animals. A little smaller than the pied wagtail, with a short tail. Summer visitor only.

Description 18 cm long. Male has a striking black and white plumage with a long tail. The female's back is greyer. (Continental race – white wagtail – has a grey back and less black around the head). These birds live up to their name, frequently bobbing the tail up and down.

Grey wagtail (R). Grey above, yellow below. Typically near water. A little longer overall than the pied wagtail, but the tail is relatively long. All year round.

Habitat Farmland, open country, towns. Often near water.
Habits Roosts in reedbeds, trees or buildings, sometimes in large numbers. Feeds by dashing at prey on the ground, or flies to catch it on the wing. Breeds mainly from April to June, laying 5-6 light grey eggs.
Sounds A loud 'tchissik' call as it takes flight.
Diet Flies, beetles, moths, other insects.
Range Widespread but leaves Scandinavia for S in winter.

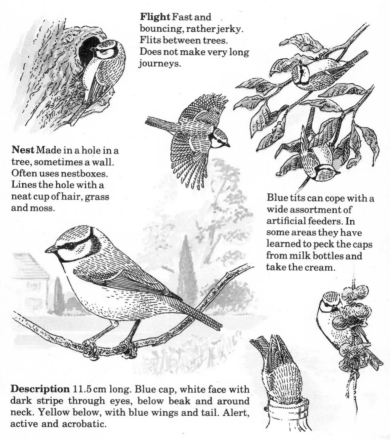

Flight Fast and bouncing, rather jerky. Flits between trees. Does not make very long journeys.

Nest Made in a hole in a tree, sometimes a wall. Often uses nestboxes. Lines the hole with a neat cup of hair, grass and moss.

Blue tits can cope with a wide assortment of artificial feeders. In some areas they have learned to peck the caps from milk bottles and take the cream.

Description 11.5 cm long. Blue cap, white face with dark stripe through eyes, below beak and around neck. Yellow below, with blue wings and tail. Alert, active and acrobatic.

Habitat Woodlands, parks and gardens.
Habits Usually in trees. Climbs on the thinnest twigs, often upside down, searching for food. Often becomes quite tame. Breeds in April and May, laying up to 15 white eggs with reddish-brown spots.
Sounds Calls a rather thin 'tsee-tsee-tsee' and other notes.
Diet Caterpillars, aphids, grubs, other insects, spiders. Nuts, cheese and fat from feeders in gardens.
Range Very common throughout, but absent from N. Scandinavia.

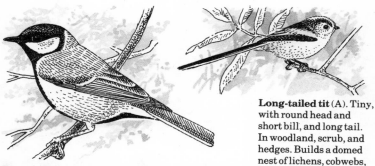

Long-tailed tit (A). Tiny, with round head and short bill, and long tail. In woodland, scrub, and hedges. Builds a domed nest of lichens, cobwebs, hair and feathers.

Description 14 cm long. Black cap, neck, chin and stripe down breast. White cheek patches. Greenish back. Yellow belly. More solid-looking than other tits.

Flight An undulating flight with a flurry of fast wingbeats.

Coal tit (A). White nape and brownish body. Very small bird. Often in coniferous woods.

Crested tit (R). Black and white crest feathers. Often in coniferous woods. In continental Europe but not Britain except part of Scotland.

Nest In a hole in a tree or wall. Likes nestboxes. A nest cup is made of moss, with hair and small feathers for lining.

Habitat Woods, parks and gardens.

Habits Searches for food in trees and bushes; sometimes on the ground. Breeds in April and May, laying 8-12 white eggs with red-brown spots.

Sounds Calls a loud metallic 'tsink-tsink', also 'teacher-teacher-teacher' and other notes.

Diet Insects, spiders, buds, some berries and seeds.

Range Very common throughout Europe.

Flight A deeply undulating flight, with wings folded between groups of wingbeats.

Nest A hole excavated in a large tree, usually well off the ground. No nesting material except woodchips.

Green woodpeckers often feed on ants' nests on the ground. Recently used ant hills may show damage. Droppings may also be nearby, containing skeletal fragments of ant within a grey envelope.

Description 32 cm long. Head with red crown and black patch around each eye. Male has small red patch below the black. Body and wings are green above, yellowish-grey below; rump is bright yellow. In flight the bird can appear yellow.

Woodpeckers have a strong chisel-shaped beak with which they can chip bark and bore into wood. They also have an extremely long tongue used to scoop up insects.

Habitat Woodlands, farmlands and heaths with trees.
Habits Climbs tree trunks with head up. Also seen on the ground, moving by clumsy hops. Breeds in April and May, laying 5-7 white eggs.
Sounds A loud laughing call, giving the bird its other name, 'yaffle'. Rarely drums on tree trunk.
Diet Wood-boring grubs and ants. Some fruits, nuts, seeds.
Range Generally common, but absent from Ireland, N. Scotland and N. Scandinavia.

Description 23 cm long. Black above, with large white wing patches, white across each eye and with other white spots. Pale underparts. Bright red under the tail. Male only has a red patch at the back of the head.

Nest A hole 3 m or more up in an old tree, often where it is decayed. The entrance hole is oval; the chamber below has no lining other than woodchips.

Flight An undulating flight typical of all woodpeckers.

During climbing, two toes on each foot face forwards and the other two, long-clawed, toes face backwards, helping to support the bird as it grips the bark. The stiff tail feathers are also used as props.

Patches of bark knocked from trees, with beak marks chiselled in the wood, are a sign of a woodpecker searching for grubs. Pine cones lodged in tree trunk crevices and looking battered are signs of woodpeckers feeding on pine seeds. Piles of battered cones may be below a tree as if suitable it is used repeatedly.

Habitat Woods of all kinds. Parks and gardens.

Habits Climbs upwards on the trunks of trees with its head up. Rarely seen on the ground. Breeds in May and June, laying 4-7 white eggs.

Sounds Call is a loud, quick 'tchik'. No song, but instead uses its beak to 'drum' very loudly and rapidly on a dead branch.

Diet Wood-boring grubs, other insects, baby birds. Also seeds, nuts.

Range Widespread and generally common, but absent from Ireland and N. Scandinavia.

Nest Usually hidden in a crevice behind bark or ivy, from 1 to 3 m up a tree. Made of dry grass, hair and bark fibres. Tufts sticking from behind bark sometimes make it obvious.

Flight Rather slow and weak; slightly undulating. Tends to follow a standard tree-to-tree feeding route.

Treecreepers have learnt to burrow or nestle into crevices in bark of introduced species of trees, such as *Wellingtonia*, to roost, thus getting some camouflage and protection from the cold.

Description 12.5 cm long. Brown upperparts, with paler streaks, silvery-white below. A thin down-curved bill. Scurries up trees like a mouse.

Habitat Woodlands, parks, gardens with trees.

Habits Searches for food on the bark of tree trunks, starting at the bottom and climbing in a jerky spiral, before flying to base of the next tree. Breeds from April to June, laying 4-7 white eggs with dark spots.

Sounds Call is a high thin 'tseeee'. Song is also high-pitched.

Diet Small insects, spiders.

Range Fairly common, but absent from N. Scandinavia, much of W. France, Low Countries and Spain.

Nest In a hole in a tree. The entrance is often plastered with mud to reduce its size. The floor is lined with dead leaves and bark fibres.

Description 14 cm long. Blue-grey upper parts with a black stripe across each eye. Whitish throat. Light brown, almost orange, below. Strong, pointed bill. In constant movement.

The nuthatch wedges a hazelnut into a crevice, then hammers it open with its beak to reach the seed. The beak may leave crescent-shaped marks in the nut. The empty nutshell is left in the crevice and the nuthatch moves on.

Flight Sudden take-off. Rather jerky, undulating flight. The wings are wide and rounded and the tail short.

Habitat Broad-leaved woodland, parks and gardens.

Habits Climbs up and down trees, and may be seen head-up or head-down, as it clings by its feet only. Sometimes seen on the ground. Breeds April to May, laying 6-10 white eggs with red-brown markings.

Sounds Rather metallic calls – 'hweet-hweet-eet'. May be heard hammering nuts.

Diet Insects. Also nuts, seeds, berries.

Range Common, but absent from Ireland, Scotland and Scandinavia.

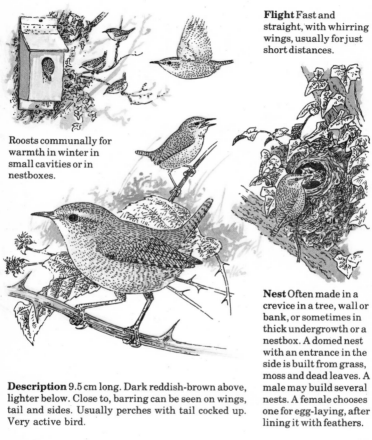

Flight Fast and straight, with whirring wings, usually for just short distances.

Roosts communally for warmth in winter in small cavities or in nestboxes.

Nest Often made in a crevice in a tree, wall or bank, or sometimes in thick undergrowth or a nestbox. A domed nest with an entrance in the side is built from grass, moss and dead leaves. A male may build several nests. A female chooses one for egg-laying, after lining it with feathers.

Description 9.5 cm long. Dark reddish-brown above, lighter below. Close to, barring can be seen on wings, tail and sides. Usually perches with tail cocked up. Very active bird.

Habitat In undergrowth and thickets in woods, scrub and well-vegetated gardens.

Habits Usually near the ground, sometimes on it. Secretive. Keeps to cover, rarely seen on open ground. Breeds from April to July, laying 5-6 white eggs with small red-brown markings.

Sounds Call is a loud harsh 'tit-tit-tit'. A loud shrill song.

Diet Small insects and their larvae. Spiders.

Range Common throughout. Some leave N. Europe for the S in winter.

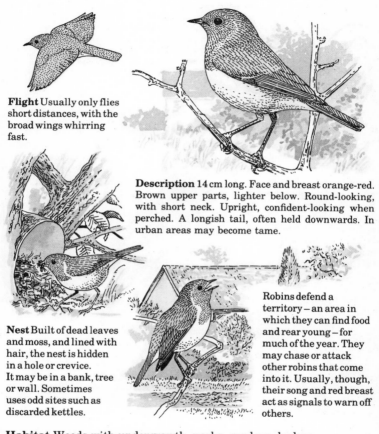

Flight Usually only flies short distances, with the broad wings whirring fast.

Description 14 cm long. Face and breast orange-red. Brown upper parts, lighter below. Round-looking, with short neck. Upright, confident-looking when perched. A longish tail, often held downwards. In urban areas may become tame.

Nest Built of dead leaves and moss, and lined with hair, the nest is hidden in a hole or crevice. It may be in a bank, tree or wall. Sometimes uses odd sites such as discarded kettles.

Robins defend a territory – an area in which they can find food and rear young – for much of the year. They may chase or attack other robins that come into it. Usually, though, their song and red breast act as signals to warn off others.

Habitat Woods with undergrowth, parks, gardens, hedges.
Habits Spends much time on the ground looking for food. Also seen and heard singing from perch in a tree. Usually aggressive to other robins. Breeds March to June, laying 4-6 white eggs with reddish blotches.
Sounds Call a sharp 'tic, tic'. The pleasant warbling song is heard all year.
Diet Insects and their larvae, worms, berries, seeds.
Range Common throughout. Leaves N. Europe for S in winter.

Nest A cup of grass, leaves, moss and plant stems strengthened with mud. A lining of grass. Usually in a bush or hedge, sometimes in a tree or ledge.

Flight May take a step or two before taking off. Usually flies low on broad wings with spread tips. The flight is direct but jerky. On landing the tail is cocked up.

Very noisy on the ground as it scuffles and prods among dead leaves for its food. Partially eaten fruit such as apples and pears, with beak marks, may show where a blackbird has been feeding. Droppings may also be stained with fruit juice, and may enclose pips.

Description 25 cm long. The male is black, with a bright yellow bill. The female is dark brown, slightly speckled below. The tail is quite long. Partly white individuals are quite common. May cock head when looking for food.

Habitat Woodlands, parks, gardens and farmland.
Habits Noisy, bold and noticeable. It spends much time on the ground looking for food. Hops and runs. Gives loud alarm call when disturbed. Breeds March to July, laying 3-5 greenish eggs with brown spots.
Sounds Alarm call is a loud 'tchuck, tchuck, tchuck'. The song is loud and flute-like, without repetitions.
Diet Insects and their larvae, worms, berries, fruits.
Range Mostly very common, but absent from N. Scandinavia.

Flight Very direct, with little closing of wings.

Nest In dense foliage in bushes or low in tree. Cup formed from grasses, stalks and moss strengthened with mud. A smooth lining of dung mixed with saliva.

Description 23 cm long. Brown above, buff below, with dark brown spots on breast. Alert appearance. Cocks head when looking for food.

Mistle thrush (B). Larger, more erect. Heavier, rounder spots. Shuts wings in flight. Does not use anvil.

May pick flesh from fruits such as cherries, leaving the stones on stalks. Smashes snails on an 'anvil' stone to get at soft parts. The shells are left lying by the stone.

Habitat Parks, gardens and woods with clearings.
Habits Often feeds on the ground in the open. May hop or walk. Breeds from March to July, laying 3-5 blue eggs with a few black spots.
Sounds Sings through much of the year. Clear musical song with repeats – 'tu-ittee, tu-ittee', from conspicuous perch. Alarm call 'tchack-tchack'.
Diet Snails, some worms, insects, fruits and berries.
Range Common, but leaves N. and E. Europe for S in winter.

Recording and surveying

One of the most important aspects of being a naturalist is keeping a proper record of your finds and observations. It may seem tiresome at first to carry a notebook with you when all you want to be doing is observing birds and finding clues to their life, but as time goes on you realize the value of a written record, however brief, of the things you have seen. It is all too easy to forget the details of even the most exciting sightings of birds, or to muddle up your finds, unless you have got a note of what is what.

The kinds of information you will want to note are
— the identity of the bird or birds you see (or a description if you do not recognize it).
— where you see it, i.e. place and type of habitat.
— when you see it, i.e. date and time of day.
— conditions, of weather and sunlight.
— what it was doing.

The best form of notebook for fieldwork is an A5 size spiral-bound reporter's notebook. Your notes do not need to be specially neat, but it is a help in recording, and using the information afterwards, to use a standard type of layout. An example of the kind of entry you might make is shown opposite.

A sketch of what you saw is very helpful if you are hoping to identify later a bird you did not recognize immediately. Draw an oval for the body, another smaller one for the head, and you can add rough outlines of wings, legs, tail and beak. In particular, mark patches of colour that you notice; this can make all the difference between a later confirmation of your suspicions and not being quite able to remember the colour of the bird's rump.

Be methodical, too, with finds such as feathers, pellets and food remains. Always carry with you on expeditions a small supply of polythene bags for your finds. The type with a press closure along the top is best. Write information about each find on a piece of paper and put this in the bag with the specimen. This is a better idea than writing on the bag itself. A quick sketch of the specimen as you found it may be useful later, and for clues such as footprints it is essential. Carry a small ruler or tape to measure prints, and record the measurements on your sketch. For some footprints, a photographic record is best of all. For this sort of work a single-lens reflex camera, with which you see in the viewfinder the actual image you are taking, is very much the best. With such a camera you can add accessories for close-up or long range work when you feel the need.

The quick notes you write in the field can be rewritten more fully in a permanent book at home. Some people like, in addition, to keep a diary of their natural history forays. Not only can these be great fun to read later, but also very informative if they include observations and feelings over a long period.

Once you get past the first stage of going out birdwatching just to see what you can spot, you may decide you would like to try a longer term project. One which you can attempt in almost any kind of country, or even in a town, is a bird census. Once you become proficient at birdwatching, there are various 'official' census schemes and standardized counting methods which you can use. But to begin with, practise in your local area counting birds or locating territories in the breeding season by marking positions taken up by male birds you hear singing. To be of interest, you need to make your observations regularly, and in a standard way, but they need not be of lengthy duration or difficult in format. You might choose to walk round the lake in your local park and count the birds. Done once, it is of minor interest, but done every Saturday morning of the year at about the same time, walking round in the same direction, may reveal much of interest about the comings and goings and waxing and waning of populations. You could choose to survey regularly along a footpath, perhaps counting the birds just to one side of it, or you might survey along a row of gardens in town, in a straight line across some fields in the country, or, more ambitiously, to try to map the birdlife in a wood.

Investigating nests

Bird's nests are fascinating objects and there is much to be learned from studying them. At the same time, it is unfair to birds, and illegal, to disturb them while they are breeding. The following suggests some ways you can investigate nests and nesting behaviour during much of the year without harming the birds in any way. Most of the observation can be carried out from a window or a seat in the garden. If you do not have a garden, try the same studies in a park or area of wasteland.

1. Nest building. In the spring, observe the birds in your garden to see what they are gathering to build or line their nests. You can help things along by providing them with a choice of nesting material. Place the items where the birds can reach them, or make a little roll of wire netting, fix it to the ground or bird-table, and tuck nesting material in it. Watch what is taken away. You can provide such materials as feathers, straw, hay, dry dead leaves, sheep's wool gathered from wire fences, kapok and so on. You can also use shredded scraps of cloth or paper, soft string or knitting wool. The latter have the advantage that you may be able eventually to trace the material you provided to a particular nest, but remember that a nest full of bright colours may attract enemies. Also be careful with artificial materials – some such as nylon thread can be deadly to birds.

As with other types of observation it is often better to make a series of regular observations for limited periods rather than one long watch. Each time you see a bird carrying probable nest material
(a) Note the species of bird. Note the material. Do different species have different preferences? Do they take materials in different proportions?
(b) Note the first dates you see a species gathering material, and the last. you may even be able to do this for individual birds. How long does the nest-building period last? Is it the same for each species?

2. Feeding the young. If you have watched the gathering of material for nests, you will also probably have noticed at least some of the nest sites in your garden or nearby. At a nest, there will be a lull in activity during the incubation period, then the parent birds will become busy again feeding the chicks. Observe the parents

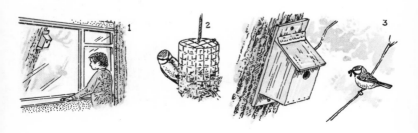

taking food to the young. (Stay well back in your observation post – you may find binoculars a help.)

(a) For each species, note when you first see food-gathering by parents, and when you last see it. How often do the parents feed the young in a half-hour period? Is this the same later on as when they first hatch, or does the frequency change?

(b) For each species note, as far as possible, the type of food carried in. You should be able to tell whether dinner consists of caterpillars, worms, centipedes or flies. (Do not feed birds at your bird-table in the breeding season. Most of the food we can provide is unsuitable and indigestible for the young). Do some species stick to particular kinds of food? How far do the parents seem to be travelling to find it? Can you estimate the quantities being used?

3. Examining the nest. After all the young have flown for the year, it is possible to examine the nest. But beware! Some birds will rear more than one brood a year if they have the chance, so it may be quite late in the autumn before you can be sure the nest is no longer in use. Once it is out of use, you can go to it and take a good look. (Most small birds build an entirely new nest each year.)

Note the shape of the nest. How is it fixed in place? Does it have a lining? What does it seem to be made of?

You can now remove the nest for closer examination. It is best to use gloves for this operation. Cut through any twigs supporting it, and lift it gently clear. It can be preserved as an intact specimen (see pages 76-77) or it can be taken apart to discover more about how it is made and what is in it. Put the whole nest into a polythene bag, add some insecticide, close the bag, and leave it for some while. This is to kill the insects which often infest nests. Later on you can tease the nest apart and find out its constituents. Some of them may surprise you.

Did any insects come out of the nest? Can you tell what they are? Are they kinds which are feeding on the birds, such as fleas, or are they just using the nest as a shelter? What is the nest mainly made of? How many metres of straw did the bird use? Can you identify any material in the nest that you provided in the spring? Has anything unusual been used, or something that must have come from some distance, or are all the materials local?

Making a bird museum
Nobody wants a room full of stuffed birds – that is not the sort of museum intended. But it is possible to set up a very good reference collection of finds of your own which will help you in identification and finding out more about how birds live. You can include in your museum feathers and other parts of birds, nests, food remains, pellets, casts of footprints, and so on. Just the sorts of clues and evidence which are discussed in this book.

Feathers. Note where and when you collected each feather. Identify, if possible, the species and position of the feather on the bird. Mount your collection in a looseleaf book. A strip of Sellotape will hold the base of each feather. A strip cut in the paper will hold the top. 'Preen' the feathers to make them look good, by using your fingers or a small brush. They should keep indefinitely in a reasonably dry place, but a little insecticide is useful to keep pests at bay.
  The larger and more comprehensive your collection the easier it becomes to identify new finds and you may become really knowledgeable about feathers. Sometimes you come across a whole dead bird – perhaps it has flown into a car windscreen – and this gives the opportunity to get sample feathers from several parts of the body to build up your collection.

Dead birds. Mounting a dead bird is a difficult and skilled operation. If you find a dead bird, you can use the feathers (as above) or some of the other parts (see below) for your museum.

Wings. These are quite easy to preserve and give a lot of information. Cut the wing from the dead bird and keep it stretched out by pinning it to a board. Within a week or so in an ordinary dry room it will be ready to be stored in an envelope or drawer. You have now got detailed information on the feathering and proportions of a wing. Try gently flapping it up and down in your hand. Which way is there less air resistance? What happens when you move it horizontally through the air? If you gradually add to your collection, you can have first-hand experience of the aerodynamic properties of different bird wings.

Feet. Feet can be preserved by simply drying them in the same way as wings. Footprints of birds can also be preserved by making plaster casts of them. It is especially interesting if you have a footprint and an actual foot of the same species to compare.

Bones. Bird bones are mostly light and fragile, but you may be able to preserve at least the larger ones and the skull. There are several ways of separating bones from a carcass and cleaning them. The carcass can just be left in a jar of water for a few weeks. This is smelly and unpleasant but the end results are good. Alternatives are simmering the carcass gently in boiling water in an old saucepan (add a little washing soda) or allowing it to be eaten away by beetle larvae or ants. Perhaps the simplest method is to put the carcass on a tile or board in a quiet corner of the garden and cover it with an old heavy flowerpot, leaving just a tiny crack for ants to get in. After several weeks the bones should be picked clean and, after bleaching with dilute household bleach, can be added to your collection.

A complete skeleton or a perfect skull is a valuable specimen. Keep the smaller bones in matchboxes, or taped to a card, and carefully labelled so they do not get muddled.

Nests. Gather nests as suggested on pages 74-75. Store them dry and whole in boxes or polythene bags. It is a good idea to use insecticide to preserve the nests otherwise they will be attacked by pests that will in time break them down. To help keep the shape of collected nests, spray them with hair lacquer.

Food remains. Collect pine cones, nuts and seeds which have obvious signs of feeding by birds, identifying the culprit wherever possible. It is useful to have examples used by squirrels and mice for comparison with the way birds tackle these foods. These items can make an attractive and informative display, either in a drawer or arranged on a board as a wall-display.

Pellets. If you find owl pellets or pellets from birds of prey, you are quite likely to find several in the same place. Some you will probably want to take apart to discover, as far as you can, what the bird has been feeding on, but it is worth preserving a few characteristic examples in a reference collection. They are susceptible to attack by moths and beetles, and some may fall apart when very dry, so it is a good idea to treat them with insecticide and spray with lacquer.

A note on hygiene. If you are handling dead birds, or parts of birds, or even dealing with insecticide, it pays to take precautions against harmful bacteria and chemicals by wearing rubber or polythene gloves. Always wash your hands thoroughly after handling biological material. It is also sensible to avoid inhaling dust from feathers, owl pellets and so on. With elementary sensible precautions you are unlikely to come to harm.

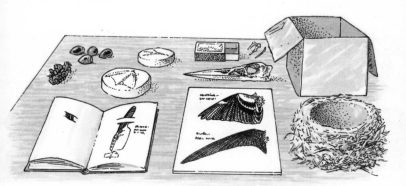

As you will have realized from this book, there is a great deal of birdwatching to be done near home. But there comes a time when you would like to see something different, perhaps some rarities or birds that only live in one part of the country, large concentrations of birds or an area rich in a particular species. The list that follows is a small selection of good birdwatching areas.

England

1. Dungeness, Kent
2. Tring Reservoirs, Herts
3. Epping Forest, Essex
4. Thetford Forest, Norfolk
5. Cley-next-the-Sea, Norfolk
6. Ouse Washes, Cambs
7. Minsmere, Suffolk
8. Dovedale, Derbys
9. Freiston Shore, Lincs
10. Cannock Chase, Staffs
11. The Farne Islands, Northumberland
12. Bempton Cliffs, Humberside
13. New Forest, Hants
14. Pagham Harbour, Sussex
15. Poole Harbour and surrounding area, Dorset
16. Dartmoor, Devon
17. Hayle Estuary, Cornwall

Wales

1. Dinas Head, Dyfed
2. Dyfi Estuary, Dyfed
3. Llanthony Valley, Gwent
4. Great Orme, Gwynedd
5. Worms Head, Gower, West Glam.
6. Holyhead Mountain, Anglesey
7. Clywedog Reservoir, Powys

Scotland

1. Cape Wrath, Highland
2. Glen More, Highland
3. Bass Rock, Lothian
4. Glentrool Forest, Galloway
5. Loch Garten, Highland
6. St Abb's Head, Borders

Ireland

1. Wexford Wildfowl Reserve, Co. Wexford
2. Bull Rock, Co. Cork
3. Loop Head, Co. Clare
4. Lough Foyle, Co. Londonderry

British Trust for Ornithology (BTO), Beech Grove, Station Road, Tring, Herts. Administers bird observatories and runs the national bird-ringing scheme. Organizes the Common Bird Census. Information and advice on fieldwork and conservation.

Royal Society for the Protection of Birds (RSPB), The Lodge, Sandy, Beds. Runs reserves, protects birds, informs and educates. A large membership. The junior wing, the Young Ornithologists' Club (YOC), is at the same address.

Wildfowl Trust, Slimbridge, Gloucestershire. (Also at Martin Mere, Lancs.) Conservation and education on all aspects of wildfowl.

The Royal Society for Nature Conservation, The Green, Nettleham, Lincoln LN2 2NR. Owns 44 trusts which together run some 1,300 reserves, many of which are excellent birdwatching sites. Total membership 140,000.

British Ornithologists' Union, c/o Zoological Society of London, Regent's Park, London NW1 4RY. Initiates and supports research work and field studies related to birds.

Bibliography

The Mitchell Beazley Birdwatcher's Pocket Guide by Peter Hayman
The Readers Digest Nature Lovers' Library – *Field Guide to Birds of Britain.*
The Hamlyn Guide to Birds of Britain & Europe by Bertel Bruun & Arthur Singer
Collins Field Guide to the Birds of Britain & Europe by Roger Peterson, Guy Mountford & P. A. D. Hollom
Book of British Birds (Readers Digest/AA).
The Popular Handbook of British Birds by P. A. D. Hollom (Witherby)
The Atlas of Breeding Birds in Britain & Ireland by J. T. R. Sharrock (BTO/IWC)
Nesting Birds, Eggs and Fledglings in Colour by Winwood Reade & Eric Hosking (Blandford)
Collins Guide to Animal Tracks and Signs by Preben Bang & Preben Dahlstrom
Watching Birds by Ian Wallace (Usborne).
Birdwatcher's Yearbook by John E. Pemberton (Buckingham Press)
Discovering Birds by Tony Soper (BBC)
Birdwatcher's Britain ed. John Parslow (Pan/Ordnance Survey)